Interview
BetterView

Interview BetterView

A Job Seeker's
Essential Guide to
Interviewing Skills

Thomas J. Franke

Roundhouse Recruiting

How will this book give you a BetterView?

Hiring managers commonly say they want to hire someone they can trust, who is dependable, likeable, and has good communication skills. Most also need to have a good "gut feeling" about the candidate... but almost none of them can specifically tell you what they look for to measure these qualities. So, knowing this in advance, how do you approach your upcoming interview?

This book can help you bridge that gap!

Inside, you will find clearly presented techniques to give you a BetterView on the types of questions you can expect to receive during an interview and how to answer them. All the interview questioning techniques are covered. You will quickly become proficient and comfortable handling any type of question. Then, we will go beyond these expected topics to provide you with a clearer understanding of what is actually occurring during an interview. The conventional thoughts about interviewing will be challenged and you will learn new techniques to really impress!

This guide is packed with useful information for even the most advanced users and the material is presented in a concise, common sense way so anyone can improve.

We will cover topics such as:

➢ Introducing a new approach called Impression Interviewing™ that will provide practical techniques for you to control an interviewer's "gut feel," your likeability, and the other hard-to-define attributes critical to obtaining that job offer.
➢ Quickly learn to handle Traditional interview questions.

- ➢ Learn to master Behavioral Interviewing. This approach to questioning has become much more common over the last 20 years and is now used by many companies.
- ➢ Understand Job Competency Models. These models create the subject matter for the different types of behavioral interview questions.
- ➢ Develop your List of Questions to Ask the Interviewer. A sample list of questions is provided along with an approach to company research.

Strategies are also included for common interviewing challenges faced by:

- ➢ New College Graduates
- ➢ Sales Job Seekers
- ➢ Technical Job Seekers Lacking Interpersonal Skills
- ➢ Managerial Job Seekers Lacking Supervisory Experience
- ➢ Job Seekers with a Felony or Misdemeanor Criminal Record
- ➢ Transitioning Military
- ➢ Senior Job Seekers

Why I wrote this book

I don't know who came up with the concept of using an interview to make critical hiring decisions which impact the lives of job seekers and influence the success or failure of companies. But whoever that person was, they did not do us any favors because they forgot to provide an instruction manual. For years, I have watched job seekers as well as hiring managers struggle to define what they are attempting to accomplish during an interview. The result is a vague exchange of information where interviewers stab blindly into the dark with their questions, important subjects get missed, and little is learned. Even worse, because few have ever taken the time to develop an effective interview method, ignorance and human nature have combined to develop the prevailing concept that interviewing is more art than science.

As a result, both the job seekers and the hiring managers of the world are suffering.

It's time to break some widely held misconceptions. It's time to break some paradigms. It's time to realize that interviewing can actually be more science than art. It's time to obtain a clearer understanding of how to approach your interview in an effective manner.

It's time for a BetterView.

About the Author

Thomas J. Franke

Throughout his career, Tom has interviewed and placed thousands of candidates in technical and non-technical positions across a wide range of industries. He founded Roundhouse Recruiting in 2008 because of his passion for growing companies and helping individuals to develop their careers. His extensive experience has encompassed all aspects of recruiting and has driven Tom to create advanced solutions to interviewing for both job seekers and hiring managers. Prior to founding Roundhouse Recruiting, Tom held in-house senior human resources management and operations management positions for Fortune 500 and leading regional companies throughout the Eastern US. He began his career as a manufacturing manager where he drove performance in both traditional union as well as non-union self-directed work team environments. His mix of experience in operations management, human resources, and third-party recruiting provides a unique depth and perspective in interviewing and recruiting. He has developed, applied, and taught job competency modeling and behavioral interviewing skills. He has been recognized as a Senior Professional in Human Resources (SPHR), having obtained his certification in 2007. He holds a dual master's degree in human resources development and management, as well as an undergraduate degree in operations management.

Connect with Tom on:
Email: tfranke@RoundhouseRecruiting.com
LinkedIn: www.LinkedIn.com/in/tomfranke
Twitter: @RoundhouseJobs
Website: www.RoundhouseRecruiting.com

Copyright

Dedication

This book is dedicated to my father, Carl Franke. After growing up during the Great Depression and graduating from high school, he volunteered to serve in WWII sailing Liberty ships for the Merchant Marines and then served in the Army. He showed me what it means to be selfless, work hard each day, and do the right thing. When I graduated from college and obtained my first supervisory job, he told me to remember the people who work for me. I have written this book for everyone who works hard to improve themselves for the benefit of their family, friends, company, and community.

Shout-Outs and Acknowledgements

I haven't told many people about this story because it's embarrassing... while I was driving to my first interview for my first real job after graduating college, my car ran out of gas! I had borrowed my brother's car to make the drive from Cincinnati to Louisville because I was afraid that my old car wouldn't make it that far. Well, I was so excited about my interview that I failed to read the gas gauge properly and the next thing I knew, the car ran out of gas on highway I-71 and I was stranded on the side of the road in the middle of nowhere. This was in 1990, before cell phones. There I was, jumping up and down in my nice new suit trying to flag down anyone who might help. Luckily for me, a couple of local guys recognized my distress and pulled over to drive me to a gas station. I still appreciate these Good Samaritans for their assistance, and I would like to thank them for helping me to get back on the road to my future. I ended up arriving to my interview an hour late, but I overcame my horrible first impression by projecting energy, optimism, and talent (all topics we will discuss later in this book) in every way possible. I was fortunate enough to receive the job offer, and I began my work as a supervisor in a manufacturing plant where my experiences would set the course for the rest of my career.

When I graduated from college 30 years ago and entered the world of work, I had no idea that I would become so passionate about recruiting, and with it, the skill of interviewing. Over time I have found that I love to learn about organizations and people and discover the match between the two. When successful, a company can experience growth and success, while at the same time, an individual can grow in their career and support their family.

The way I approach my work began during my childhood. I was blessed with my loving parents, Carl and Shirley, and relatives who instilled my most important qualities which still drive me today. I cannot thank them enough for their support and for setting an example through the ways they approached their personal and professional lives. In this same way, I would also like to thank my brother Ted and sister Carla, for supporting, loving, and challenging me throughout my life.

During my career, I have had the opportunity to learn from observing many different work styles from a long list of managers and coworkers across many very different types of industries. Some of my managers were excellent, some were just average, a few were unethical, and some were clearly incompetent. However, I learned from them all, and I would like to acknowledge and thank them for the opportunity and experience.

Lastly, I would like to thank my wife Kristen for her love, support, insight, and wonderful editing skills. I was blessed when I met her a few years ago and she has changed my life. She brings more joy and excitement to me than I could have ever imagined.

Table of Contents

CHAPTER 1: How to use this Book

BetterView is about exploring and advancing your understanding of the practice of interviewing. Each chapter is packed with useful information for even the most advanced users, and the material is presented in a concise, common sense way so anyone can improve.

The subjects contained in this book are essential and comprehensive. We begin by looking at interviewing through the perspective of the interviewer. Truly understanding what the interviewer desires enables you to adjust your approach and be successful in your interview. Then all the interview questioning techniques are covered. You will quickly become proficient and comfortable handling any type of question. Next, we will go beyond these expected topics to provide you with a clearer understanding of what is actually occurring during an interview. The conventional thoughts about interviewing will be challenged and you will learn new techniques to really impress! You will develop a strategic approach to company research and create your list of questions for the interviewer. Advice for common challenges are also presented. Finally, you will develop an approach to successfully accomplish your primary objectives in your interview. Each chapter will build upon the previous one, beginning with basic questions and then moving to advanced concepts.

Overview of the Upcoming Chapters in this Book:

Chapter 2 provides an understanding of the priorities and objectives from the perspective of the interviewer. This information will give you the clarity to focus successfully on your approach and the actions needed to meet the interviewer's expectations.

Chapter 3 introduces you to the many different types of interview questions. An overview of the Job Match, Traditional, and Behavioral questions is provided. Then, other important aspects of interview questions are discussed, so you will be able to understand employers' varying approaches to questions and handle unintentional and ineffective questions.

Chapter 4 discusses Job Match questions. These are the initial go/no-go questions you must overcome in order to be considered a legitimate candidate and advance to the next stages of the interview process.

Chapter 5 lists many of the different Traditional interview questions you may be asked. Strategies are included to assist with answering each question. Eight different categories of traditional interview questions are covered such as strengths and weaknesses, and there are even questions for managers.

Chapter 6 is the first of three chapters on Behavioral Interviewing. In this chapter you will learn in depth about what behavioral interviewing is and how it is used by interviewers. You will learn how to give 3-part Situation – Action – Result answers. You will also learn how the question and answer exchange works between you and the interviewer. This high level of understanding will provide confidence when you need to respond to behavioral interview questions.

Chapter 7 is the second chapter on behavioral interviewing. The concept of Competency Models is introduced in order to understand the role they play in developing behavioral interview questions. Understanding each of the competencies provides you with the subject matter needed to develop your list of situational examples for the different behavioral questions you will be asked.

Chapter 8 brings competency models and behavioral interviewing together in the third and final chapter on this approach. An extensive list of behavioral questions is presented for 16 different competencies. Answering these questions will provide you with excellent practice for your upcoming interview. You will also develop a strong list of situational examples through your preparation with these questions.

Chapter 9 challenges you to take a new perspective in how to approach interviewing by introducing the Impression Interviewing technique. The clarity provided by this approach will allow you to develop new skills to improve all aspects of your interview. These impressions are the method to separate yourself from other candidates and obtain the job offer.

Chapter 10 provides a detailed understanding of impression interviewing. You will learn different types of impressions and how to use them to excel in your interview. Controlling your different impressions, in areas such as charisma and talent, will allow you to control the initial and lasting impressions perceived by the interviewer.

Chapter 11 gives the insight and tools needed for you to make the most of your opportunity when the interviewer allows you to ask questions. Developing a strategy for your questions is discussed. Then, an approach to company research is presented. Sample questions for you to ask are also included.

Chapter 12 provides strategies for seven of the more common challenges faced by job seekers such as new graduates, sales candidates, and senior candidates. This very specific and practical information clarifies the challenges these different groups will face in their interviews. Then strategies to overcome these challenges are presented.

Chapter 13 is the final chapter of this book and will refocus and prepare you to be successful with the primary objectives in your interview.

Each aspect of interviewing is covered thoroughly so that you can understand the concept, develop your approach, and improve your skills. Sample questions and answers are also provided for your practice and preparation. As you work through each chapter and build your interviewing skills, I think that you will also find that the more you learn about interviewing, the more you will come to understand that there is still more to know.

Preparation earns Consideration

I have personally conducted interviews with over 10,000 candidates during my 30+ year career working as an operations manager, then HR manager, and then as the owner of a recruiting firm. During this time, I have been consistently shocked by the lack of preparation from the vast majority of candidates. It has continued to amaze me that the majority of job seekers just show up for an interview unprepared. Then these same candidates are surprised, sometimes even offended, when they are told that they are not receiving a job offer.

Conversely, it is quickly obvious and refreshing to interviewers when they are presented with a candidate who has taken the time to prepare. Preparation is a sign of respect and demonstrates that the candidate genuinely values the interview process, company, as well as the interviewer. In return, interviewers will give more attention, time, and consideration to those who have prepared. These same candidates are also the ones who consistently receive more and better job offers.

Confidence comes from Preparation

Do you get nervous before your interview? A few butterflies and excitement are normal, but if you become extremely nervous, it's because you did not prepare sufficiently for your interview.

This book covers the different types of interviewing skills in depth so you can improve your performance in an interview immediately. However, if you truly want to become a superior interviewer, you will take the time to prepare and then practice on an ongoing basis.

Interviewing is not a natural skill acquired at birth; the best interviews come from practice.

You will separate yourself from the other candidates by using this book to prepare and practice. Your preparation will appear as confidence and will lead to making that unforgettable "WOW" impression!

CHAPTER 2: From the Interviewer's Perspective

In order to be successful in your upcoming interview, it will benefit you greatly to first understand the perspective of the interviewer. This chapter will provide you with insight to comprehend and appreciate what interviewers are looking for in today's job market.

In this book I refer frequently to the job titles "hiring manager" and "interviewer." These titles do not always mean the same thing, so let me describe what is meant by these terms. The hiring manager is the person who ultimately makes the decision to extend an employment offer, and this person will usually become your direct manager. The interviewer may also be the hiring manager, but usually is a different person within the organization, such as an internal recruiter, HR supervisor, or office manager, who will conduct an initial interview as a preliminary screen for the hiring manager.

The Interviewer's Calendar

You, the job seeker, can most simply be described as a block of time on your interviewer's calendar.

Even before your interview happens, much effort has been put forth by the hiring manager and interviewers to fill their opening. Your interview is actually one of the later steps in the process. First, approval is needed to authorize the position. A job description and advertisement must be written and posted. Additionally, the position pay range was requested and approved, a workspace set up, and an interview procedure developed. Candidates must be sourced and resumes reviewed. Your resume was most likely not the first received, and frequently, hundreds of resumes have been received and reviewed before interviewing of candidates even begins. During this time, the hiring manager and his department have also been overworked because they were shorthanded.

So now that you have received the invitation for your initial 20-minute phone interview, you need to realize that you will have just a few minutes to make a positive impression and earn consideration for your desired position.

Managing the Interview

In all your interviews, from the initial phone screen to the final interview, it is commonly accepted that the interviewer will lead candidates through the interview. He will have his list of questions that must be answered, and his schedule, which needs to be maintained. Because this is the common practice, he will also expect to be the leader. Therefore, your best approach is to relax, let the interviewer lead the discussion, and focus on providing clear answers with energy and optimism. Conversely, if you attempt to control the interview, your actions will be interpreted as overbearing and disrespectful.

Focus your answers on topic to meet the interviewer's needs. Staying on topic will earn you respect and consideration as the interview progresses. Even if the interviewer doesn't specifically ask a question on a topic you want to discuss, there will be enough open-ended questions where you can communicate your strengths. Every topic will eventually be covered. Your objective is to ensure that the interviewer continues to remain interested so that you can move to the next step in the selection process.

What Kinds of Impressions Will You Make?

Hiring managers today want what they refer to as "well-rounded candidates." This means that they want to hire a person with strong technical skills, strong interpersonal skills, and also that "WOW" factor, which is that wonderful feeling or impression made during the interview. When they talk with candidates, they want to find the person who has everything. They are going fishing and just like everyone else, they want to land the biggest fish in the sea! This desire has been described in a number of ways, such as:

- Are you a "Well-Rounded Candidate?"
- Do you have the "It-Factor?"
- Do you have the "X-Factor?"
- Will the hiring manager like you?
- Will the hiring manager have a good "gut feeling" about you?
- Are you a "Star Candidate?"

With this expectation in mind, now you need to find a way to stand out and get the interviewer excited about you.

The challenge here, which we all have come to realize, is that most hiring managers do not really know how to define and measure these "WOW" attributes, and since they do not know what they are looking for, how in the heck are you supposed to know what to show them? What should your approach be to meet these vague and lofty expectations?

The answer is actually straightforward, and the lessons taught in this book will enable you to master these "WOW" attributes! You can learn to impress your interviewer, but it will require some preparation on your part. You will also need to open your mind to a new perspective of what is really happening during an interview.

Begin by researching the company and practicing your responses to the job match, traditional, and behavioral interview questions. Your ability to effectively handle these questions will demonstrate that you meet the requirements for the position.

However, there are a lot of candidates who meet the requirements for the position, so if you really want this job you will need to show more and prepare in a different way beyond traditional thinking. You will need to show your charisma and talent through the many ways you communicate. You will need to learn the different types of impressions taught in this book. You will learn to control and project these impressions and become that well-rounded candidate in the eyes of the interviewer. Throughout your interview, from before the introduction to after the closing, you will send numerous impressions. Whether you answer a traditional interview question or a behavioral question, you always send these impressions. These impressions will add color, energy, and emotion to your statements. These impressions are critically important to your success because they impact the way the interviewer feels about you! These impressions create the "WOW" factor that the interviewer is looking for from you.

In this chapter, I presented you with insight into the mind of the interviewer. This understanding provides the perspective needed as we move forward. Over the next 9 chapters, I will describe the different aspects of an interview, including the many types of questions you can expect to be asked. When you keep the interviewer's perspective in mind, you will be able to successfully construct your answers, stand out, and persuade the interviewer to be excited about you.

CHAPTER 3: What was the Question?

You would expect that in the same way different managers possess a wide range of management styles, there would also be a wide range of interviewing styles. It is remarkable to recognize that this is really not the case. The structure of the interview has remained consistent over time. Interviews begin with a brief introduction. Then, the interviewer asks you a lot of questions. Next is the opportunity for you to ask a few questions. Lastly, you wrap up the interview when the questions are completed. Almost every employer follows this same structure. The greatest difference between interviews is in the types of questions being asked.

This chapter presents all the different types of interview questions you may encounter. Three types of questions planned by interviewers are introduced. These are intentional questions effectively designed to obtain information about your overall fit for the position. Then, additional important considerations regarding questions are discussed, such as differences between employers' questioning techniques, ineffective questions, unintentional questions, and questions for you to be prepared to ask.

Types of Interview Questions

These are questions designed by the interviewer to evaluate your experience, knowledge, skills, abilities, and competencies for the position. The questions are separated into three unique categories. They have been classified as Job Match, Traditional, and Behavioral.

Job Match Questions

These questions are primarily asked during the initial interview to determine if you are a basic match for the job. The questions are straightforward. The interviewer wants to determine as quickly as possible if you are a match with the job responsibilities, if you can carry a conversation, and make a positive impression. These questions also include an overview of your previous work experience and fit with the work environment. Initial phone interviews, scheduled for 20 to 30 minutes, are mostly job match questions used by the interviewer to determine if it is worthwhile to schedule a more thorough, in-person interview with the hiring manager. Examples of job match question topics include: eligibility to work in the country, drive time to work, ability to travel, basic position responsibilities, education requirement, experience summary, and hours of work.

Your goal during the initial job match portion of the interview is to get past the job match questions so that you can earn an invitation to a second interview where you can have more in-depth discussions with the hiring manager. Your answers to these questions are mostly the communication of your experience summary and other simple responses. You need to keep your answers concise and be sure to make a memorable impression. During second and follow-up interviews, which are typically on-site and last one hour or longer, you will find that there will be a little time spent finalizing any remaining job match questions, and then the interview will shift to more in-depth traditional and behavioral questions. Chapter 4 will examine these job match questions further.

Traditional Questions

If your interviewer does not know how to use the behavioral interviewing technique, then most of the interview questions you will be asked fall into this category. Most companies still depend on traditional questions as their primary selection tool.

Traditional interview questions are standard questions about you. Most of these questions are open-ended to elicit a full response. The topics covered by traditional questions are varied. Traditional interview questions ask about subjects such as: applicable work experience, strengths and weaknesses, goals and career progression, ability to work with others, supervisory skills, how you approach your work, and there are even some non-work-related personal questions. Chapter 5 will review traditional interview questions in depth.

Behavioral Questions

More and more companies are learning to ask behavioral interview questions instead of the traditional questions. This technique produces more accurate and useful information about how a candidate will perform in a job, so it is also a great benefit for you to learn this technique. Behavioral interviewing uses initial questions and follow-up questions to obtain details from specific situations in the candidate's past. The basic concept with these questions is past performance will predict future behavior.

Your responses to behavioral questions will be 3-part answers detailing a situation or experience from your past that will provide insight to how you will perform in a similar situation in the future. Chapters 6,7, and 8 thoroughly teach the behavioral interviewing technique. Learning how to answer behavioral questions is an important skill that can also be used to improve your answers to all the other types of interview questions.

Important Considerations for Interview Questions

In addition to the three types of interview questions introduced above, there are additional, important considerations for interview questions. This section examines these additional aspects to interview questions in order to prepare you fully for your interview.

Differences between Employers

Most employers, especially at smaller companies, lack prepared questions to evaluate their candidates. These interviewers and hiring managers have topics in their minds they want to discuss, but most of them just shoot from the hip and make up the questions on the spot. Obviously, this is not a thorough approach. These may be very well-run companies with developed systems in other parts of their operations, but for whatever reason, they just have not developed their interview process. For these interviews, you need to be proactive in communicating your strengths and skills because the interviewer may not specifically ask you about everything. Therefore, it is your responsibility to tell them what they need to know about you. The interviewers who lack prepared questions also rely more heavily upon the impressions you project, and put less emphasis on your actual answers to questions.

The employers with prepared questions will assign topics to each interviewer to be sure to cover. They frequently also use behavioral interviewing and an interview guide, including a specific list of questions for each interviewer to ask. In the organizations using prepared interview questions, both your answers to questions and the impressions you project are significant factors in the hiring decision.

Speculative Questions

A speculative question asks how you would or how you should do something. Some interviewers ask speculative or theoretical questions on purpose, but most ask these questions unintentionally when they phrase a question incorrectly. Speculative answers are only opinions or theoretical musings. These answers lack useful information about your actual job performance, so interviewers really should avoid asking these questions.

Responses to speculative questions use the words "usually," "would," "could," or "should." The best way for you to answer a speculative question is to give a behavioral answer.

Situational Questions

This is another form of a speculative question that needs to be avoided. By asking a situational question, the interviewer wants you to hypothetically put yourself into a work situation to ask what you would intend to do. These types of questions do not produce useful answers about how you have really performed in your job in the past.

Responses to situational questions also use the words "usually," "would," "could," or "should." The best way for you to answer a situational question is to give a behavioral answer.

Leading Questions

This type of question is asked in a way that leads you directly to the desired answer. An example of a leading question is, "Are you a hard worker?" and the obvious answer to this question is "yes." Interviewers ask leading questions by mistake and the question needs to be rephrased in order to solicit useful information.

The best way to answer a leading question is to give a behavioral answer.

Open-Ended vs. Closed-Ended Questions

Most of the questions asked by the interviewer will be open-ended in order to allow a full and open answer from you. Your response should be complete with some detail, but not excessively wordy. Remain concise and efficient with your answer. The interviewer will ask a follow-up question for additional details if he needs this information.

Closed-ended questions typically are asked at the end of a discussion topic to check facts and confirm understanding. Your responses to these closed-ended questions should be very brief and to the point. The only exception to this rule is whenever you notice that the interviewer has asked you a leading or closed-ended question by mistake and it is clear that he is really looking for an open-ended response from you. This is a common error made by interviewers who have just phrased their question incorrectly. In these instances, you should respond with the brief immediate answer to the interviewer's closed-ended question and then ask the interviewer if he would like for you to provide an example of when you have handled a similar situation in your past. This response will help the conversation to flow properly and also show your strong judgment by politely recognizing the interviewer's mistake and offering additional information to answer his question.

Are you an Excessive Talker?

If you naturally have the ability to give a 30-minute answer to a yes or no question, be aware that this is an extreme detriment in an interview. The most hated candidate for interviewers is the person who will not shut up. Excessive talking blocks the interviewer from asking you important questions and makes the interviewer very uncomfortable because he has lost control of the interview. As soon as the interviewer realizes that you are a talker, he will stop trying to learn about you and then politely interrupt you so that he can halt your interview and not lose time with the next candidate scheduled on his calendar. This is why, especially during the initial interview, providing short, concise answers is helpful. Otherwise, you will be left to wonder why the interviewer only asked you one question before hanging up the phone.

How can you Prepare for Every Question?

The answer to this question is simple; you do not need to prepare for every question. Instead, a comprehensive approach is to prepare for each competency. In chapters 7 and 8, you will learn about the different types of competencies and how to prepare your list of situational examples. This method of preparation will arm you with flexible answers so you will have a strong, positive response to any type of question.

How you Answer is Important

Whenever you answer any of these different types of questions, it is important to realize that in addition to your answer, you are also projecting multiple impressions to the interviewer. Your eye contact, posture, and the energy in your voice are a few examples of the impressions you are projecting. These impressions mean just as much as the words you say. Chapters 9 and 10 will prepare you for impression interviewing.

Questions for You to be Prepared to Ask

After the interviewer has finished asking his list of questions, it is time for you to be prepared to respond with questions of your own. This opportunity for you to ask questions should not be an afterthought, because this is the only time during the interview when the interviewer will relinquish control and allow you to choose the discussion topics. In chapter 11, you will learn how to develop your strategy and prepare your list of questions for maximum positive impact.

Now you have reviewed and become familiar with all the different types of interview questions. The following chapters examine job match, traditional, and behavioral questions in greater depth. When you have fully prepared for your interview by using the techniques presented in this book, you will confidently welcome any type of interview question.

CHAPTER 4: Job Match Interview Questions

As a job seeker, you need to be aware that Job Match interview questions begin immediately after the introduction. These are straightforward go/no-go questions, with answers required before the interviewer will give you serious consideration. Interviewers try to obtain answers to these questions as soon as possible, usually during a phone screen or the initial interview.

Many of these job match questions are derived from the job requirements for the position, as listed in the job description. These job requirements are the minimum knowledge, skills, and abilities needed to successfully perform the position's responsibilities. If you do not have the job description, the job advertisement is also a good source for you to obtain this information because it usually lists the most important job requirements. Prior to your interview you will want to read the job advertisement and job description in depth. These documents provide a lot of valuable clues about how much of a match you are for this job and what knowledge, skills, and abilities the interviewer will be looking for during the interview. In addition to these minimum job requirements, the job match questions also evaluate your previous employment and work environment to determine fit with the position. Here are some examples of the different types of job match questions you may encounter:

Job Requirement Questions

These questions primarily come from the knowledge, skill, and ability requirements listed in the job description for the position.

1. Are you legally eligible to work in this country?
2. How far is your drive to work? Do you have transportation to work?
3. Are you open to relocation?
4. Are you willing to travel? How much?
5. Are you able to work the scheduled hours? Can you be available to work overtime, evenings, or weekends?
6. What type of position are you applying for?
7. What is your education? Degrees completed?
8. What certifications have you completed?
9. What computer software skills do you possess?
10. What is your desired compensation?
11. Can you lift 25 lbs.?
12. Do you have two years of previous customer service experience?
13. Can you type 40 wpm?

Past Job Experience Questions

As part of the job match, questions about your past job experience are asked to determine how this position fits with your career progression. Be prepared to answer these questions for each of the positions you have held in the past.

1. Are you currently employed? If no, why not?
2. What was your position title?
3. To whom did you report?
4. What were your job responsibilities?
5. What duties from your current job do you enjoy the most/least?
6. Did you have client contact?
7. What was your pay rate?
8. What do you like about your current company/position?
9. Why did you leave this company/position?

Work Environment Questions

The interviewer wants to understand how much of a match you are with the organization's work environment and culture.

1. What do you know about our company?
2. Why do you want to work here?
3. What type of work culture do you desire?
4. Describe your work style.
5. What are you looking for in a company?
6. Are you a match with our dress code?
7. Are you comfortable working on a construction site?
8. Are you comfortable working in a large office environment?
9. Are you comfortable working in a self-directed work team environment?

Your objective during the job match questioning is to give clear information to quickly confirm that you are a match for the job, enabling the interviewer to think that he is speaking with a legitimate candidate. Once you give the interviewer confidence that you are a "match," then the questioning will transition to the more in-depth subjects. In the next four chapters we will study these more advanced traditional and behavioral interview questions.

CHAPTER 5: Traditional Interview Questions

Here are some examples of common traditional interview questions you may be asked during your interview. For each question I have also provided some suggestions and insight to assist with your answers.

Questions on Goals and Career Progression

Why are you looking to leave your present position?
Give a clear, simple reason for wanting to leave and then be sure to state what you are looking for in your new company. Be positive on this subject and avoid any negative comments about your present supervisor, company, and co-workers. Stress the positive things you experienced, but then let the interviewer know that it is time for you to move on and you see this new position as the right match. Your answer should be concise so you can quickly move onto the next question.

Can you tell me about yourself?
Your answer needs to be concise. Give a brief overview of your education, experience, and objective for your job search. Emphasize your relevant experience and why you are a fit for this position. Then ask, "Is there anything else about me you would like to know?" You do not know if the interviewer is looking for any specific subject areas so this question will give him the opportunity to define and restate the question more accurately.

What are your short-range goals?
Your goal is to find an opportunity where you can be challenged and experience success for yourself as well as helping to make a positive impact on the performance and success of your team and company.

What are your long-range goals?
You want to grow with a company, learn more about the business, have the opportunity to apply your skills, and be an asset to the company. As you develop your skills, you would like the opportunity to be given additional responsibilities.

Where do you see yourself in five years?
You do not know the company well enough to say where you would see yourself in five years. As you work hard and develop your skills, there will be opportunities where you can contribute to the needs of the company in the future.

How long will you plan to stay with us?
Your objective is to find a company where you can fit and build your career long term. Even though the vast majority of people change companies during their careers, this is not the time to discuss it and employers do not want to hear it.

Why do you want to work for us?
This is a great open-ended question giving you the opportunity to mention the research you did on the company and how your strengths match with their needs.

What types of positions/companies are you considering?
You want to mention other similar position titles and industries. Do not give specific company names and stay on subject with the interviewer's company. The interviewer is looking for consistency, so do not mention any other types of positions showing a different career path. Be brief so you can move onto the next question.

What are your monetary requirements?
Some companies will put off any salary discussion until they are interested in making an employment offer, some companies will want to know an initial salary range, and a few will want to pin down a specific pay rate as soon as possible. Your strategy here should be to put off specifics on salary until you are extended an offer. Once an employer states that they want to extend an offer then you will have more power in the salary discussion, so this is the main reason why you want to delay. You will also want to clarify your job responsibilities, to whom you will be reporting, and other compensation such as benefits, commission structure, or bonus structure that will impact your total compensation. A response to the salary question can be, "At this time, I am really looking for an opportunity that is a match with my skills so I am

be interested in discussing salary later, once we have determined this is a good fit for me as well as for the company." If they do push you for some idea of salary, give them a range as opposed to a number. Make it a generic range, such as the mid $70s depending upon total compensation, and stress that the match with the position is most important to you.

This position pays less than what you have made in the past, so what makes me think that you will stay and not leave for a position that pays a little more?
You will want to stress that the match with the job responsibilities, relationship with your manager, and company culture are the most important to you.

Are you overqualified for this job?
The interviewer may ask this question to determine if you will stay in this position or jump at the next opportunity, if you will demand a higher salary than they want to pay, or if you may not be open or trainable to their way of doing things. Respond by asking clarifying questions to determine what the interviewer is really wanting to know, and then address the specific concern. Emphasize that this position is a match with your needs, your loyalty and desire for a long-term match, and your adaptability to different ways of working.

Your experience is light for this position, so why should we hire you?
For this type of question, you will want to emphasize your strengths that are not trainable, such as your work ethic, and then emphasize your ability to learn when given new responsibilities. Be prepared to share specific examples from your past where you have taken the initiative to learn new skills and quickly become productive.

Why haven't you been promoted?
This is a vague question for which you have no answer, so refocus the discussion onto the position at this new company. Promotions come from positive company performance, individual performance, and being in the right place at the right time. Most of these factors are outside of your control and you just want to do well in this current position.

If you could be anywhere right now, where would you be?
State that this position and organization look to be a strong match for you so there is not anywhere else where you want to be right now.

Questions on Strengths and Weaknesses

<u>What have been the three biggest accomplishments in your career so far?</u>
The interviewer wants to know why you are a stronger candidate than any others. Answer this question with the behavioral interviewing approach, as described in a later chapter. Relate your situations as closely to the job as possible. Make sure they are true accomplishments, and not job responsibilities.

<u>What are your strengths?</u>
You should name strengths that relate to the job. Be prepared to give examples with the behavioral interviewing approach.

<u>What are your weaknesses?</u>
This is a great opportunity to talk about how you turned a weakness into a strength. Again, use the behavioral interviewing approach to phrase your answer. Examples may be how you learned a new skill, how you became a subject matter expert, or earned respect as a leader.

Questions on Your Ability to Work with Others

Have you ever had difficulty working with a supervisor or manager?
<u>How well did you work with your previous supervisor?</u>
Keep your response positive and do not criticize your previous supervisor, no matter how bad your past situation. Emphasize your approaches to maintain open communication with your supervisor. Give examples of how you asked for constructive feedback and supported directives or initiatives from your supervisor with others.

<u>Who have been your mentors?</u>
This is more of a question about your ability to learn. Discuss skills you have learned that are harder to define such as how you have learned to work with others, how you have improved your judgment in vague situations, and the business ethics you have developed. If you have never had a good mentor, you can express your desire for one so that you can continue to learn.

Do you prefer working on a team or alone?
The answer is both. Individual as well as team skills are necessary to be successful in any position.

What do people most often criticize about you?
This is another question where you can show how you have turned a weakness into a strength. Do not share a major flaw. Instead discuss something minor or less shocking. An example topic may be your initial lack of industry knowledge. You can share how you took the initiative to turn your industry knowledge into a strength.

What do you expect from a supervisor?
A few desired supervisory skills are leadership, being given clear expectations, and independence to perform without being micromanaged. Emphasize your maturity and ability to work with little direction.

Questions on How you Approach your Work

How do you measure success?
The success of the company is #1 so the company's measures are your measures. Then, the success of your department is #2. Your individual success is #3. If you are successful in performing your responsibilities while being ethical and doing things the right way, then this is the best way for you to impact the organization.

What makes you unique?
This can be rephrased to, "What strengths can you bring to our company?" Share attributes and skills that you consider to be your personal strengths. Your answer should also match with the needs for this position and company. You can personalize your answer by sharing some history on how you developed your strengths.

What kinds of things do you find to be annoying or irritating at work?
Again, you want to keep your response positive so try to avoid too much detail in your answer to this question. An effective approach is to talk about your ethics at work, putting forth effort and doing the right things help to create a positive culture and performance.

What ethics do you bring to work?

All interviewers want someone who is trustworthy and ethical, but unfortunately, questions pertaining to ethics are almost never asked in an interview. There are a few reasons for this avoidance. One reason is that conversations on ethics are usually limited to macro, big picture philosophical discussions. The more useful micro-ethics discussions where you are asked to share your personal ethical challenges escape evaluation. Most interviewers have never been asked about their personal ethics, so it is not even a subject in which they are familiar. Therefore, ethics becomes a vague, undefinable subject they do not know how to approach during an interview. Another reason is that ethics is one of the less tangible attributes, so it does require greater effort to develop appropriate interview questions. As a result, for most interviewers, ethics might as well be dumped into that ambiguous pile with all of the other "soft skills."

Now, you would clearly like for your interviewers to know that you have solid ethics, but what do you do when your interviewers lack the ability to ask any questions on this subject? The first step is to prepare some situational examples to share from when your ethics have been challenged at work. If you think about it, everyone has their ethics challenged daily in a work setting. Examples can be as simple as not taking excessive lunch breaks, putting forth genuine effort, doing the right thing when others are not watching, or following company policies. Next, you should look for opportunities during your interview to briefly insert your ethics examples. The best opportunities can come from open-ended questions that allow for you to give a wider range of responses. Because ethics is rarely brought up in interviews, just you mentioning the word will make a positive impression on the interviewer.

Questions for Supervisors/Managers

How comfortable are you supervising people?
If you have never supervised anyone, then I suggest that you seek out someone you respect who has some supervisory experience and ask as much as you can about supervising others. Supervision is a set of learned skills. People are not born to be good supervisors.

The most effective supervisors work in alignment with company and department values. They do not ignore situations and they take the initiative to identify and address performance issues in a constructive way. They understand that proactively holding conversations with employees on difficult subjects helps to build trust and fosters improvement over the long term. If you are comfortable taking on this responsibility, then you will learn whatever is needed to be a successful supervisor.

Have you ever fired someone? How do you use a performance improvement plan?
The main purpose of this question is to determine if you know how to administer progressive discipline. You can answer by giving an example from previous experience where you needed to progress through a few steps of discipline. The strongest answer will include examples where you provided the support, training, and tools necessary for success, but the employee still failed to perform, with no excuses. If you have never fired an employee, share your knowledge of the progressive disciplinary process.

How do you deal with employees who have a bad "attitude?"
An effective supervisor manages work performance behaviors, not attitudes. You will find that attitudes are not listed in the employee manual performance management section. This is because an attitude is hard to measure and supervise, whereas a behavior is measurable and actionable. Behaviors include actions such as what an employee does or doesn't do, and what an employee says.

How do you challenge your good employees to do better?
Performance improvement comes through regular discussions with employees about their roles in the company. Proactively setting goals, then coaching, then feedback instills an environment of continuous improvement. Prepare examples of specific employees and the discussions you have held with them to share.

What would your employees say about you?
Emphasize your ethics and performance with respect. Then refer the interviewer to ask some of your former employees about you. Include a few of these employees on your List of References so the interviewer can easily speak with them.

Personal Questions

These questions do not have anything to do with your job match or ability to perform the required responsibilities, so answer politely and briefly; then refocus the discussion to the job. You want to respond in a way that gives the interviewer confidence that you are open, well-rounded, and likeable, so keep your answer positive in tone. Be concise and move on so you can avoid the risk of bias coming from an answer where the interviewer has a different personal preference than you. Some of the non-work-related questions you may be asked are:

- What do you like to do in your spare time?
- What is your favorite book and why?
- If you could be any animal, what would you be?
- What are your hobbies?
- What's your favorite TV show?
- Are you a democrat or republican?
- How would your friends describe you?

The Wills, Woulds, and Shoulds

Any question beginning with, "would you…," or "how should you…," is a speculative question. This means that you are being asked to speculate on something in the future. These types of future-oriented questions elicit vague responses and provide no insight into how you actually perform in a job. Does the interviewer really want to hear your theoretical musings on how one should be a good team player at work? No! He just wants to know if you are a good team player. Interviewers ought to avoid these types of questions and, "stay away from the woulds," but sometimes they just do not know how to properly phrase a question. So, when you are asked this type of question, your best strategy is to turn the question into a behavioral interview question, and then give a specific answer detailing what you actually did in the past. This approach provides insight to the interviewer as to how you have performed on the job, as well as a specific story, leaving a tangible memory with the interviewer. Behavioral interviewing is covered in a following chapter.

How would you rate yourself as a professional?
Turn this into a behavioral interview question. Can you give me an example of when you responded to a situation in a professional manner?

How will you earn respect from your team?
Turn this into a behavioral question. Tell me about a time when you earned respect from your team.

Would you describe yourself as a team player?
Turn this into a behavioral question. Can you give me an example of when you were a good team player?

What would you have done differently in your career?
Turn this into a behavioral question. Can you tell me about a time when you did something differently in your career?

Would you consider yourself to be detail-oriented?
Turn this into a behavioral question. Give me an example of when you had to be detail-oriented.

Other Common Questions

<u>What do you know about our company/position?</u>
The interviewer wants to know how much you prepared and if you are a fit with the company. Do your homework in advance, focusing on the company and the specific position. You should be able to find a wealth of information on the internet about the company, its owner(s), and competitors. You can also research the people you will be interviewing with, so you can familiarize yourself with their pictures, or find common ground such as the type of degree or school attended. The best research is finding and talking with any current or former employees. Company research is discussed in more depth in a later chapter.

<u>Who are our competitors?</u>
The interviewer wants to know if you have done your company research. You should research the company's competitors and share specific information demonstrating that you have learned about this industry. You should also take this a step further by being able to have an introductory discussion on the strengths and weaknesses of the competition and how the company you want to work for can strategically compete. You are still a novice and outsider, so do not pretend to be an industry expert; you just want to show that you have the potential to think tactically.

<u>How did you prepare for this interview?</u>
Your advanced research and preparation will demonstrate your interest, work ethic, and planning skills to the interviewer.

<u>What have you been doing since you were laid-off? / Why did you have a large gap in your employment?</u>
Emphasize that your time has been spent searching for a company and position that are the right fit. The interviewer will also want to know that you aren't lazy, so mention the family responsibilities, home improvement projects, or other productive tasks that have kept you busy during this employment gap.

<u>Why do you want to go back to work for someone else after being a contractor/independent business owner?</u>
This is a difficult question and you will need to take the time to thoroughly answer. Many managers do not want to hire someone who has been used to making as many or more strategic decisions as they have, and many fear that you may be too

independent to be supervised. The easiest initial answer here is that going back to work as an employee will allow you to focus on the part of the job you love, and not burden you with all the other time requirements of running your own business. You will then want to follow up by asking if the hiring manager has any specific concerns with you on this subject, so you can directly address each of these concerns. Obviously, anyone who has been self-employed brings a diverse skill set, experience, different type of confidence, strategic view, and strengths as compared to someone who has never worked independently. This will give you a lot of positives you can bring to your new employer. The hiring manager wants to have confidence that you will stay at the company and be a team player.

<u>Why should we hire you over other candidates?</u>
You do not know who your competition is and you should not care to know. The strongest response is to emphasize why you are the best person for this job and bring the conversation back to your past performance, and your energy and passion that you will bring to this position.

CHAPTER 6: Understanding Behavioral Interviewing

Behavioral Interviewing is an interviewing technique used to predict a candidate's future performance by asking for specific examples of how the candidate has acted in similar situations in the past. The concept can be simply stated as, "Past performance predicts future behavior."

For hiring managers, behavioral interviews provide a more structured approach and produce better information about a candidate, as compared to traditional interviews. This approach has become much more common over the past 20 years. Some companies have now formalized behavioral interviewing as part of their interview process, with different sets of interview questions developed for the most common positions. You can now find companies that train how to conduct behavioral interviewing, and you can even become certified as a behavioral interviewer.

For you, the job seeker, I have found that understanding how to answer behavioral interview questions is also very advantageous today. Most people may have heard of behavioral interviewing, but few really understand the questioning approach used by interviewers, or how to provide the 3-part behavioral responses. Learning how to answer behavioral questions is easy, so this chapter will give you a BetterView of behavioral interviewing and enable you to stand out in an interview for both behavioral as well as other types of traditional questions.

Situation - Action - Result

A behavioral interview question begins with the interviewer asking you for an example of something you have done in the past. Then, when you answer a behavioral interview question, your response should always consist of these 3 parts:

> **Situation-** First, describe the situation, challenge, or task you faced.

> **Action-** Second, state what action(s) you took in that situation.

> **Result-** Third, tell what the result(s) were from each of your action(s).

It is really that simple, and with some practice and preparation, you will be able to cruise through your interview. Another advantage is that the interviewer will recognize your interviewing skills. He will appreciate that you know what you are doing because he will not need to ask you as many follow-up questions.

Now let's review behavioral interviewing in more depth so you can really learn to master this approach.

Behavioral Interviewing Q&A Exchange

The question and answer exchange between you and the interviewer is predictable. After answering a behavioral question, you need to listen carefully to the interviewer for any follow-up questions. If the interviewer restates the same question in a different way, then you probably gave a vague response and the interviewer is looking for a more specific answer. If the interviewer asks, "What did you do?" or "What did you say?" then you were probably vague in describing your actions. If the interviewer asks, "What was the result?" then you probably did not specifically describe the result(s) in your response. Interviewers are trained to ask their initial behavioral question, then listen for your response, then depending upon how complete your answer was, they will respond in one of three ways. This exchange is detailed here:

First, the Interviewer asks you a behavioral question.

Then you respond with:

1) **A Complete Answer** (This is your desired outcome, providing full detail on the Situation, Action, and Result)

2) **A Partial Answer** (You missed some detail on the Situation, Action, or Result)

3) **A Vague Answer** (Your answer was off topic or too vague without any Situation, Action, or Result)

Then the interviewer responds to you in one of these three ways:

1) **For a Complete Answer-** The interviewer will ask a follow-up question to obtain another situational example from you, or he will move onto a different topic.

2) **For a Partial Answer-** The interviewer will ask follow-up questions to get a complete Situation, Action, and Result from you.

3) **For a Vague Answer-** The interviewer will restate his original question in order to obtain a useable answer from you.

Your responses to behavioral questions should be concise and efficient. Each response should last no more than one or two minutes at the most. If the interviewer would like more detail about a subject, he will ask a follow-up question. Responses should also stick to the topic and not wander off on different subjects. Vague answers that are not relevant to the question should be avoided. The failure to stay on topic shows a lack of attention and poor judgment. Let the interviewer guide the process.

As we just learned, follow-up questions from the interviewer are asked when you failed to provide enough detail in your answer on the Situation, Action, or Result. It is common for the interviewer to ask follow-up questions for more information, so do not consider their additional questioning to be a negative sign. They expect to ask these follow-up questions. Now here is some more good news- The different types of follow-up questions you can expect to be asked are also very predictable! They are almost always open-ended questions, so you have leeway to respond with a complete answer. Here are some examples of follow-up questions you will be asked by the interviewer:

Follow-up questions asked by the interviewer for Missing Situations:
1. So, what was the situation?
2. What task were you doing at that time?
3. Describe the circumstances you were dealing with.
4. Describe what led up to that.
5. Give me a specific situation where you used that approach.
6. What was the most memorable time when that happened?
7. When was that?

Follow-up questions asked by the interviewer for Missing Actions:
1. What action did you take?
2. What did you do?
3. Exactly what did you do?
4. How did you react?
5. What was your response?
6. What did you say to him?
7. Describe specifically what steps you took.
8. Walk me through the steps you took.
9. What was your part of the project and how did you handle it?
10. What did you do first?... second?...

Follow-up questions asked by the interviewer for Missing Results:
1. So, what was the result?
2. What was the outcome?
3. How did it work out?
4. What feedback did you receive?
5. What were the results from your actions?

Important Considerations for Behavioral Interviewing

It is common for interviewers to ask follow-up questions to obtain more detail about a situation, and you should continue to keep answers concise and on topic. This will enable the interviewer to decide when to ask for more information, and it will keep the conversation flowing smoothly.

Now, you also need to realize that just giving a complete answer to a behavioral question is not enough. Your answers need to be based on strong positive situations from your past, presenting your skills and capabilities in the best light. The interviewer is looking for positive answers from you, so a lack of preparation beforehand can lead you to provide some weak experiences from your past because you can't remember anything better to share at that moment.

A few days prior to your interview, you will want to take some time to think of strong situational examples you can use to respond to each of the different types of behavioral questions. Topics will come from the job advertisement or job description for the position, and also from the list of competencies we will discuss in the next chapter. Taking this time in advance of your interview to develop your situational examples list is very important because you will then be able to quickly recall your strongest answers.

What should you do if you lack experience and do not have a situational example for a question? Remember that the interviewer is trying to understand your ability within a certain competency, so his objective is to obtain multiple situational examples to assess this competency. Therefore, you can provide an answer to a related situation that will suffice. Also, if you look at the competencies in the next two chapters, they all describe skills you have been exposed to in some way during your life. The competencies are trying to assess your capabilities in work performance, communication, problem solving, and leadership. You will find that every person, no matter how old, will have more than enough experiences from work or personal life to provide insight on all of these competencies.

Let's take a moment to talk about honesty in your interview. It is very difficult for a candidate to lie in a behavioral interview. Also, lying or embellishing will never be as impactful as an honest answer from personal experience. A good interviewer will dig for genuine, meaningful responses that produce emotion and passion from a candidate. In these situations, it is difficult to make up plausible stories when you are repeatedly being asked follow-up questions for details. Almost everyone has "tells" such as talking in circles, vague responses, tripping over words, lack of eye contact, or nervous shifting and arm movements, so a lack of honesty will be revealed. Everyone should have enough strong examples from their past performance to be able to shine in an interview, so take the time to prepare examples from your past, and then your knowledgeable approach to this process will serve you well. Your personal examples are also the best ones to use because your passion, pride, and energy will show when you speak of your challenges and accomplishments.

While the basic concept of behavioral interviewing is simple, another interesting aspect of this process is that being a candidate and answering the behavioral questions is actually easier than being the interviewer and having to ask them. Many interviewers struggle with knowing when and how to phrase follow-up questions. It is not very natural for interviewers to ask the appropriate follow-up questions. As a result, during your interview you may notice that you will receive a few leading, closed, or speculative questions as your interview progresses.

The most common challenge candidates have when answering behavioral questions is avoiding vague, theoretical, or speculative responses. Instead of providing a specific example in their response, candidates sometimes reply with a generic response such as "In that type of situation I generally," or "I usually," or "You should," or "I would." Stay away from these types of vague responses and focus on providing specific Situation – Action – Result examples from your past experience. Interviewers are trained to identify these inappropriate responses, and they will respond by restating the question for you to start over again.

Whether you received a poor question from the interviewer, or you veered into the "woulds" and shared your opinion instead of an example from your past, this situation is always solvable. You can gain some bonus points in your interview by recognizing when this happens and then adjust your response to give a proper Situation – Action – Result answer. Here's a little practice for these situations. Turn these speculative and leading questions into proper behavioral questions:

Turn these Speculative Questions into Behavioral Questions:

1) What makes you think you are good at solving problems? (Answer: Give me an example of a time when you solved a problem.)

2) Can you describe what a good team member should do? (Answer: Tell me about a situation when you showed that you were a good team member.)

3) How would you handle a conflict with a co-worker? (Answer: Tell me about a time when you had a conflict with a co-worker.)

4) How do you usually find new prospects? (Answer: How do you find new prospects in your current position?)

5) How do you typically plan your day? (Answer: How did you plan your day yesterday?)

Turn these Leading Questions into Behavioral Questions:

1) I guess you found being a team leader to be very fulfilling? (Answer: Tell me about a team leading skill which you developed for yourself.)

2) Would you say your decision to take a pay cut to keep from relocating was the toughest you had to make? (Answer: Tell me about a tough professional decision you had to make.)

3) So, it sounds like you closed the sale? (Answer: What was the outcome?)

4) When you caught this person breaking the rules, did you just drop it or did you report it to your manager? (Answer: Tell me about a time when you discovered that a co-worker was breaking the rules.)

5) Are you a hard worker? (Answer: Tell me about a time when you had to work exceptionally hard.)

Congratulations! Now you have learned the concept of behavioral interviewing, follow-up questions, the 3-part Situation – Action – Result answers, as well as the importance of preparing your situational examples list in advance. You have also gained some insight on how interviewers are taught to conduct behavioral interviews, so you should feel comfortable with knowing what to expect. In the next chapter, we will discuss competencies and behavioral signs, and how they are important in behavioral interviewing. Then, in the following chapter I will show you actual behavioral interview questions. These questions are divided into groups by the different competencies critical to a position. Taken all together, the information in these three chapters will bring your knowledge of behavioral interviewing to an advanced level, and you will be excited to use these skills in your next interview.

CHAPTER 7: Job Competency Models

Behavioral interviewing has proven to be an effective approach for obtaining information about how a candidate has performed in the past. But exactly what information does a hiring manager really need to learn about you in an interview? What behavioral questions can you really expect to be asked?

This is where job competency models come into play. Competency models describe the information needed for a candidate to be successful in a job. Each competency contains behavioral signs, that are the markers, or data points, the interviewer looks for to identify the existence of these competencies in a candidate. Or in other words, competency models give an interviewer the ability to know which behavioral questions need to be asked for a specific position.

What is a Competency?

Here is a definition of a competency for our use in interviewing:

> *A Competency is a term developed by a company that is used to describe a desired knowledge, skill, trait, or attribute.*

Each person has some competencies they are born with and others that can be developed over time through life experience or the ability to learn and adapt. For example, some people are naturally more outgoing than others, so this trait will be little impacted by training. Conversely, decision-making is a skill learned and perfected through training and practice. Other competencies, such as persuasiveness, are interesting combinations of traits a person is born with plus skills learned through training.

Some competencies are easy to see and measure, such as how fast someone can run, the ability to use a hammer, or the ability to lift 25 lbs. A resume also lists some of the more obvious competencies such as education, computer skills, and experience within a particular industry or position. Other competencies are more difficult to see such as ethics, confidence, the ability to learn, persuasiveness, or resilience.

When a company develops a competency for a position, a title for that competency is created along with a definition used to describe the desired components they have identified as crucial for success. Here is an example definition for the "Drive" competency:

> *Drive- Consistently maintains a high level of energy and efficiency. The ability to keep functioning effectively and remains focused under pressure.*

Some people have more drive than others, so this competency may be a strength for some candidates and a weakness for others. Ideally, a job candidate will have strength in all the competencies identified as essential for a position, but in reality, no one is perfect, so candidates will have a mix of strengths and weaknesses.

What is a Competency Model?

A competency model is just a group of competencies assembled by a company for a specific position. Each company can develop a unique competency model for every position within their organization, so you can have different competency models for the operations manager, receptionist, IT administrator, customer service representative, and maintenance technician roles. There are also no rules as to how many competencies are needed to form a model; it really only depends on what each company has determined as necessary for their purposes. A competency model usually contains approximately 6 to 15 of the most important competencies identified as critical for an employee's success in that role.

For ease of use, these competencies can then be arranged or grouped into separate "families" such as:

1) Leadership
2) Communication
3) Performance
4) Problem Solving

Once a competency model has been developed, it then becomes a useful tool in identifying the necessary experience, knowledge, traits, and attributes that should be asked about during an interview. Because these competencies are developed by hiring managers to clarify what is required for a position, a specific list of interview questions can then be developed to obtain situational examples from candidates' past performance in similar situations. This list of questions is called an Interview Guide. Current employees can also use competency models to measure their capabilities and identify the areas they can work on to develop and improve their performance.

Here is an example competency model for a sales representative position. As you can see, the competencies have been grouped into three families: communication, performance, and problem solving. The leadership family is not needed in this example because this position does not supervise others.

Sample Competency Model for a Sales Representative:

Communication Competencies:
1) Persuasiveness- The ability to influence the decisions and behavior of others through convincing communications.

2) Customer Service- Demonstrated attention to satisfying one's external and/or internal customers.

3) Relationship Building- The ability to develop and maintain partnerships with others inside or outside the organization who can provide support.

Performance Competencies:
4) Results- Setting challenging goals, focusing effort on those goals, and taking the initiative to meet or exceed them.

5) Drive- Consistently maintains a high level of energy and efficiency. The ability to keep functioning effectively and remains focused under pressure.

6) Planning- Carefully prepares for projects and meetings, demonstrates detail and thoroughness, follows up with others.

7) Ethics- Demonstrates an awareness of business ethics. Acts in a responsible, reliable, and trustworthy manner.

8) Confidence- Faith in the ability to be successful. Shows independent thought and is comfortable deviating from others.

9) Adaptability- Openness and the ability to search for new methods and change approach in response to outside influences.

Problem Solving Competencies:
10) Tactical Thinking- Analyzing one's strengths and weaknesses relative to competition. Anticipates consequences and takes appropriate action to be prepared.

11) Decision Making- Uses a logical, systematic approach to problem solving. Gathers relevant information needed to define a situation. Anticipates outcomes and adjusts for potential impacts.

12) Business Knowledge- Possesses and develops knowledge and skills within their industry. Recognized as a subject matter expert.

What is a Core Competency?

The term "core competency" has become widely misunderstood and misused, so let's take a moment to clarify the definition. Core competencies are a small set of competencies, such as professionalism, customer service, and ethics, that an organization or department identifies as important, regardless of the job or position held in that group. In this instance, a company is stating that professionalism, customer service, and ethics are listed and required in every job competency model for every position within their group, including those in very different positions such as the operations manager, receptionist, IT administrator, customer service representative, or maintenance technician. A core competency is not "core" to a person; it is a common competency required within a group.

Behavioral Signs

A competency with its definition is helpful but it lacks the detail needed to really identify its presence, so we use behavioral signs to verify the existence of a competency.

> *A behavioral sign is something a person does or says that points to the existence of a competency.*

This is how you see a competency within a person. They are excellent tools to identify the needed behaviors for a competency, especially for the less obvious competencies. For example, the most persuasive salespeople in a company can be interviewed and studied in order to identify what they do differently to make them so persuasive. These actions set them apart and can be defined as behavioral signs to look for in other candidates. Here are some examples of behavioral signs we can observe in candidates with a strong persuasive competency.

These behavioral signs are observable in persuasive candidates:

1. Understand the sales process and apply it consistently.

2. Seek objections in order to overcome them.

3. Use stories to create images and make messages more impactful.

4. Seek personal information to use to make the purchase decision fill an emotional need.

5. Study competition to identify their product's strengths and weaknesses, and then leverage their strengths in product presentations while deemphasizing weaknesses.

6. When they hear "no" they do not stop selling. Instead, they identify this as just another objection to be overcome in order to get to "yes."

Using Competency Models in Behavioral Interviewing

Once these behavioral signs have been identified for each competency, they can then be converted into questions to use with the behavioral interviewing technique. This gives an interviewer the ability to ask for situational examples from a candidate's past to verify or nullify the existence of each of the necessary competencies in a position's competency model.

Let's convert the behavioral signs for persuasiveness into behavioral interview questions:

1. Understand the sales process and apply it consistently – Converts to: Can you give me an example of a time when you utilized the sales process?

2. Seek objections in order to overcome them – Converts to: Tell me about a time when you worked to overcome an objection.

3. Use stories to create images and make messages more impactful- Converts to: Can you tell me when you have used a story to help make a sale?

4. Seek personal information to use to make the purchase decision fill an emotional need- Converts to: Can you tell me when you have made a purchase decision emotional for a customer?

5. Study competition to identify their product's strengths and weaknesses, and then leverage their strengths in product presentations while deemphasizing weaknesses- Converts to: Tell me about a time when you used information about a competitor's product in your sale.

6. When they hear "no" they do not stop selling. Instead, they identify this as just another objection to be overcome in order to get to "yes"- Converts to: Tell me about the last time a customer told you "no."

The answers to these questions will clearly separate the persuasive candidates from those who lack this competency. The most effective interviewers have developed interview guides containing behavioral interview questions for each of the behavioral signs they have identified for the competencies in their competency model.

Here are further examples of Behavioral Signs converted to Behavioral Interview Questions for some of the other competencies:

1. Job Knowledge- Keeps current with the latest technology- Converts to: How do you keep current with the latest technology in your position?

2. Ethics- Is loyal to employer- Converts to: Tell me about a time when you were loyal at work.

3. Decisiveness- Makes decisions with limited information- Converts to: Give me an example of when you had to make a decision with limited information.

4. Results- Makes sacrifices to be successful- Converts to: Tell me when you had to make a sacrifice to be successful.

5. Resilience- Overcomes obstacles- Converts to: What was a significant obstacle you needed to overcome in your last position?

6. Persuasiveness- Develops urgency in a customer's purchase decision- Converts to: When have you created urgency in a purchase decision?

7. Human Relations- Develops relationships with difficult co-workers- Converts to: Tell me about a time when you developed a work relationship with a difficult co-worker.

As you can see, in this chapter we went into a lot of depth for you to learn the concept of competency models and the role they play with behavioral interviewing. This is actually advanced material, beyond the amount of preparation found at most companies today. Now that you have developed your understanding to this advanced level, you will be pleased to know that you will be prepared and comfortable in any behavioral interview setting.

You will need to do some preparation to answer these behavioral questions properly with your strongest situational examples. You can develop an effective list of situational examples by writing down brief notes on two or three of your past experiences for each of these competency areas. This will enable you to respond quickly and concisely to most of the questions. In the next chapter I will share example behavioral interview questions for many different competencies. You can use these questions as a guide to develop a comprehensive list of situational examples.

CHAPTER 8: Behavioral Interview Questions

In the two previous chapters you learned about behavioral interviewing and job competency models. In this chapter we will bring these subjects together. A sample competency model with 16 different competencies is presented along with behavioral questions for each competency. Sample answers and advice are also included so you can have a well-defined approach to prepare for the behavioral questions you will encounter in your interview.

The sample competency model we are using has 16 commonly used competencies, so the structure and questions will be helpful to everyone. We will call our sample model, "The Job Seeker's Competency Model."

The Job Seeker's Competency Model:

Performance Competencies
1) Results
2) Resiliency
3) Self-Confidence
4) Adaptability
5) Character
6) Planning

Communication Competencies
7) Customer Service
8) Persuasiveness
9) Relationship Building

Problem Solving Competencies
10) Decision Making
11) Tactical Thinking
12) Business Knowledge

Leadership Competencies
13) Vision
14) Performance Management
15) Employee Development
16) Team Building

Performance Competencies

The family of performance competencies includes Results, Resiliency, Self-Confidence, Adaptability, Character, and Planning. Getting results and doing it in the right way is ultimately what any job is about, so be sure to emphasize your ability to get results throughout your interview. Finish all your situational answers with strong, positive results. Self-confidence can also be described as being proactive and optimistic. Resiliency is difficult for most interviewers to assess in an interview, but this is a powerful trait that will drive success, so look for opportunities to share examples of this competency. In this same way, also look for opportunities to share examples of your character competency.

Sample Question:
Describe a time when you were particularly busy. What kind of hours did you work? How did this affect you?

Sample Answer:
(Situation)- In college, I maintained a full course load while working over 20 hours per week in two part-time jobs.

(Action)- I worked a construction job during my time off on weekdays; then on the weekends I worked in retail at the mall. I studied early in the morning and also during the evening almost every day.

(Result)- I enjoyed being busy. I maintained a 3.5 GPA, improved my retail sales skills, and learned as an apprentice carpenter. I was energized to accomplish more with my busy schedule.

Communication Competencies
The family of communication competencies includes Customer Service, Persuasiveness, and Relationship Building. These competencies define the "soft skills" such as interpersonal skills, written, and verbal communication. Relationship building and customer service are important for both internal and external relationships. Persuasiveness is the most important competency for sales professionals.

Sample Question:
When you started work at your last position, what did you do in your first few days and weeks to establish a good working relationship with your co-workers?

Sample Answer:
(Situation)- I had four co-workers in my last position.

(Action)- I wanted to earn a reputation for being dependable, so I made sure to arrive early and stay late every day. I also worked at a fast pace to show a strong work ethic. I developed new relationships with each of my co-workers by being friendly and approachable. I greeted and recognized them whenever possible. I also asked just a few questions to learn a little information about their families or interests, so I could make a personal connection. Even though I was busy, I also looked for any opportunity to offer my help to my co-workers. I also would ask my co-workers for feedback and advice.

(Result)- My approach worked very well, and I have developed and maintained a wonderful relationship with my co-workers. My timeliness and hard work earned a reputation for being dependable. My co-workers appreciated my willingness to help, and I saw my approach create an environment where everyone became more helpful. Trust was built by being approachable and then maintaining confidentiality. Asking my co-workers for feedback and advice showed my respect for them and enabled me to learn the work very quickly.

Problem Solving Competencies

The family of problem solving competencies includes Decision Making, Tactical Thinking, and Business Knowledge. These competencies focus on your ability to obtain information, evaluate it, and then make decisions. Your situational examples for these competencies need to be decisive. This means that your decisions need to be accomplished in a timely manner to meet deadlines. Tactical thinking is your ability to consider the future implications of decisions you are making today. Judgment is another term used to describe tactical thinking. Business knowledge is the sum of your knowledge, skills, and abilities within your industry or area of expertise.

Sample Question:
Tell me about a time when you acquired additional knowledge or skills in your last position.

Sample Answer:
(Situation)- In my last position I was assigned to a new department as a Project Manager.

(Action)- I observed and asked questions to identify who was the most knowledgeable expert in our department. Then, I volunteered to assist him with his projects so I could learn from him.

(Result)- The relationship was a win-win. He was able to complete projects faster and I became known as the new expert in our department!

Leadership Competencies

The family of leadership competencies includes Vision, Performance Management, Employee Development, and Team Building. These are the skill sets of informal leaders, supervisors, and senior managers. Both leadership and management skills are included in these competencies.

Sample Question:
Can you give me an example of how you have managed the performance of one of your employees?

Sample Answer:
(Situation)- I supervised an employee who was new to my department. She had a reputation for always being disciplined for her poor attendance. She was a great worker but was habitually late arriving to work.

(Action)- I met with her on the day she arrived in my department. I told her that she had a reputation for always being late and that one day something serious would happen and she would lose her job. I told her that poor attendance was unacceptable in my department and I would be watching her. Unless she took responsibility to change, I would enforce the disciplinary process and she would lose her job. I also told her to think about the consequences of being unemployed as a single mother. Then, I told her that she also had a reputation for being intelligent and a good worker, so I wanted her to be successful as an important member of our team. I scheduled monthly meetings with her so she knew that she needed to face this problem. Over the next few months, I made sure to speak with her every day about her attendance. Most days needed just a brief comment, but we discussed the problem immediately whenever she was late.

(Result)- She wasn't perfect but her attendance improved significantly and she was proud of the change. She did well with my work group. Eventually, I was transferred and we lost contact with each other. A few years later, we ran into each other and she gave me a huge hug! She told me that she never would have kept her job without our experience and while her attendance still wasn't perfect, it was no longer a problem.

Confidence comes from preparation. In this next section, practice behavioral questions are listed for all 16 competencies in our Job Seeker's Competency Model. By taking the time to prepare your 3-part Situation – Action – Result answers for each of the following questions, you will gain a clear understanding of the different subjects you will be asked about during your interview and become more comfortable with the concept of behavioral interviewing. I encourage you to keep track of the different situational examples you use when answering these questions. These situational examples will include your greatest challenges, achievements, and efforts from both your personal and professional life.

Performance Questions

1) Results

    a. Give me an example of how you have taken initiative in your last/current position.

    b. How do you decide when you need to take initiative in your work? Give me an example.

    c. Can you give me an example of when you did more than was required in your job?

    d. What goal in your career are you the proudest of having achieved? Tell me the goal and what you did.

    e. What goals/responsibilities did you have in your last position and what did you do to achieve them?

    f. What's the toughest goal you have ever set for yourself?

    g. What goals have you set for yourself recently and what are you doing to achieve those goals?

    h. In your past position, what responsibilities did you enjoy the most? What did you enjoy the least? How did you approach the work you enjoyed the least?

    i. As a sales representative, you are frequently in a "feast or famine" mode. Tell me about a time when you had a lot of business and then very little business. How did you approach these times?

    j. What is the hardest you have ever worked to succeed in your job? How often do situations call for that kind of effort? How did you feel about having to work that hard?

    k. Describe when you were particularly busy at work. What kind of hours did you put in? How did this affect you?

l. How many customers have you had in the sales process at one time? What kind of hours were you working? How did you maintain your effectiveness?

m. The end of the month is typically a busy time for a salesperson. Tell me about the last time you had a "race to the finish." What challenges were you dealing with and how did you handle them?

n. Tell me about a time when you were given responsibility to complete a project. How did you go about getting the job done?

o. There is frequently pressure to sacrifice quality in order to get your work done. Tell me about a time this happened to you. How did you handle the situation?

p. What goals do you have in your current position? What are you doing to achieve those goals?

q. Tell me about a time when you faced a lot of obstacles completing a project. What did you do?

2) Resiliency

a. Tell me about a stressful time you have had at work. How did you deal with that situation?

b. What does being resilient mean to you? Give me an example of a time when you have been resilient and what did you do to "bounce back."

c. What kinds of sacrifices have you made in order to become successful?

d. Tell me about a time when you were criticized at work. How did you respond?

e. How do you deal with stress in your current position? What do you do to reduce or prevent stress?

f. We all have times when the responsibilities of our jobs are overwhelming. Give me an example of a time when you felt overwhelmed at work. How did you react?

g. Working with customers can be challenging at times. Describe one of the most stressful interactions you've had with an internal/external customer. How did you react?

h. Sometimes interacting with others at work can be difficult. Describe the most stressful interaction you've had with your manager/supervisor/team leader or a peer/team member. How did you respond?

i. How much time are you away from home because of work? Give me an example of a time when you were away for a long time. How did you react to this?

j. Can you tell me about a time when you faced unreasonable sales goals or performance expectations? How did you deal with the situation?

3) <u>**Self-Confidence**</u>

    a. Tell me about a difficult period in your life and how you dealt with it. How did that time in your life shape the way you approach things today?

    b. In your current position, what do you do to present yourself in a competent manner to your customer?

    c. Tell me about a sale that went wrong. What did you attribute it to?

    d. Tell me about a time when you disagreed with your manager's decision. How did you react?

    e. Describe the biggest professional risk you've taken. What information did you consider before taking action? What happened?

    f. Describe a time when you supported someone else's idea that was unpopular. Why did you support the idea? What happened?

    g. Tell me about a challenging task your manager asked you to complete. How did it make you feel that your manager asked you to complete this task? How did you approach it? What was the result?

    h. When was the last time you were competitive? Another time?

    i. Tell me about the most competitive situation you have ever experienced at work. How unusual was it for you?

    j. What was the most improbable goal you have had at work/school? How was this goal established? What were your chances for success? What did you do? What was the result?

4) Adaptability

    a.   In your current position, what did you do during your first few days and weeks to adjust to your new responsibilities?

    b.   Tell me about the last procedure/computer/technological change you had at work. What was the change, what did you think about it, and how did you adjust?

    c.   Tell me about a time when you had to adjust your approach to deal with a change in the work environment or situation. What did you do?

    d.   Tell me about a time when you had to adjust to rapidly changing priorities in your department or organization.

    e.   Tell me about one of your accounts where the key contact changed. How long did it take you to establish an effective relationship with your new customer? What actions did you take?

    f.   We often have to make changes when our methods are no longer effective. Tell me about a time when you had to change your approach or method of work on an assignment or project. What did you do? What were the results?

    g.   Working with people from diverse backgrounds can be challenging. Tell me about a time when you faced a significant challenge working with people from different organizations or cultures. What did you do? What was the result?

    h.   Going from high school to college can be a dramatic change. Tell me about a particular challenge you faced when you made this transition. What did you do?

5) <u>Character</u>

    a. What is something in which you believe strongly? Why? Tell me about a situation where you were asked to do something at work that was in conflict with this belief.

    b. What is your code of ethics or value system in how you interact with your co-workers/manager/customers? Have you ever been in a situation where your ethics were challenged? Tell me what the situation was and how you dealt with it.

    c. Give me an example of a time when you received criticism from your boss. What did you do with the information?

    d. In your current/past position, what have you done to build trust with your co-workers/customers?

    e. In your current position, what kind of information do you deal with that you would consider to be confidential? Tell me about a time when you were dealing with a confidential matter. What did you do? Tell me about a time when confidence was broken and how did you respond?

    f. Would your co-workers consider you to be reliable? Give me an example of a time when you showed your reliability.

    g. Tell me about a time when you were betrayed by a co-worker. What did you do? How did that affect your relationship with that person?

6) **Planning**

 a. What is your approach to follow-up with customers? Tell me about a specific customer and how you conducted your follow-up.

 b. Tell me about a time when you had a follow-up meeting with a customer. How did you prepare for that meeting?

 c. Tell me about a time when you faced conflicting priorities. How did you determine the top priority?

 d. When you are given a complex set of tasks to accomplish, what is the process you use to complete the tasks? Give an example.

 e. In your current position, how do you organize yourself on a daily basis? Weekly? Monthly?

 f. How do you organize yourself to make sure that you meet all your objectives in your current position?

 g. Tell me about a time when you had to coordinate various resources to complete a complex project.

 h. What do you do in your current position to ensure that you produce quality work?

 i. How do you organize your files? What information is in each file and how is each file organized?

Communication Questions

7) Customer Service

   a. Tell me about a difficult customer you had to deal with and how you handled the situation?

   b. Tell me about a time when you were confronted by an emotional or angry customer. How did you respond?

   c. Tell me about a time when a customer came to you with a problem. What was the situation and how did you respond?

   d. What is your approach to ensuring that a customer is satisfied with his or her purchase? Give me an example.

   e. How do you ensure customer satisfaction throughout the sales process? Give me an example of how you handled customer satisfaction with a recent customer.

   f. In your current/last position, how did you find out how satisfied your customers were with the service/product they received?

   g. Tell me about a time when you had to do follow-up work with a customer concern. How did you follow up with this customer?

   h. What is the most fun you have ever had winning a customer over?

   i. What have you done in the last 30 days to deepen relationships with your key customers?

8) **Persuasiveness**

a. Tell me about a time when you had to be particularly persuasive with a customer.

b. Do you use a sales process? If so, describe the basic steps. Tell me about a specific customer and how you handled the sales process from the initial contact through to the close of the sale.

c. Tell me about a time when a customer told you "NO." How did you respond?

d. Have you ever used visuals, stories, or analogies to be persuasive with a customer? Give me an example.

e. Have you ever made a purchase decision personal or emotional for a customer? Tell me what you did to make it an emotional decision.

f. Tell me about a time when you created a sense of urgency with a customer.

g. Tell me about a recent customer you have had. What questions did you ask to determine the customer's needs?

h. How do you determine the decision maker in a group or family? Give me an example.

i. How do you determine what type and frequency of follow-up to use with a customer? Tell me about how you handled follow-up with a recent customer.

j. Tell me about a situation where you had to influence a peer to cooperate with you.

k. Tell me about a time when you were able to convince someone to do something he or she was initially reluctant to do. How did you convince him/her?

9) **Relationship Building**

a. When you started work at your last position, what did you do in your first few days and weeks to establish a good working relationship with your co-workers?

b. Tell me about a time you were angry with a boss, co-worker, or friend and how you handled it.

c. What do you do to develop a relationship with your customer? Give me an example.

d. Tell me about a time when you needed to approach a co-worker about a sensitive issue. What was the situation and what did you do?

e. Describe a time when you participated with someone outside your team/department/group in an activity that turned out to benefit both teams/departments/groups. What was your role?

f. Sometimes it is not easy to identify opportunities that benefit multiple departments. What have you done to find new opportunities to cooperate with another department? Give me a recent example.

g. Getting people outside your work area to cooperate often requires them to commit time for your benefit. Tell me when you asked someone outside your work area to commit time for your benefit. What did you say to gain his or her cooperation?

h. What have you done to promote collaboration and cooperation in a way that supported the overall objectives of the company?

i. Partnerships are not indestructible. Describe what you've done to sustain a healthy, productive partnership with someone.

j. What have you done within the last 30 days to deepen relationships with key co-workers?

Problem Solving Questions

10) Decision Making

a. Tell me about an important decision you made in the past that took some time to work through so I can see your approach to decision making.

b. Tell me about a decision you made where you had to consider pros and cons.

c. Tell me about a complex problem you faced which had multiple issues. What was your approach?

d. Tell me about a situation where you had to make a critical decision in a short period of time with limited information.

e. Describe your approach to problem solving and give an example.

f. How did you choose your college/major?

g. In this position you will be required to make sound decisions in highly stressful situations. Describe a previous experience where you have done this.

h. Tell me about a time when you had to make a decision in an ambiguous situation.

11) Tactical Thinking

    a.   What are some of the common customer service issues with the product you currently sell? Tell me about a recent customer and how you prepared to address these issues.

    b.   In your current position, who are your main competitors? What are the strengths and weaknesses of your product/service in comparison to the competition? Give me an example of how you have used this information with a customer.

    c.   Tell me your reasons for your job changes. What did you like/dislike about those positions?

    d.   Tell me about a risk you took recently. What steps did you take to understand the potential benefits and consequences of your action? What happened?

    e.   Describe a time when you recommended a plan of action in response to business/market trends. What information did you use to make your recommendation? Was the plan executed? What was your role?

    f.   How did you determine the ways in which you marketed your product/service? How did you measure the success of your marketing efforts? How did you decide how to adjust your marketing efforts over the long-term?

12) Business Knowledge

a. Think of a person who is very close to you and knows you well. What would that person say is an area in which you need to develop?

b. Tell me about a time when you acquired additional knowledge or skills in your last position.

c. Give me an example of a time when you learned from a mistake.

d. Give me an example of when you used a new marketing method in your last position.

e. What are some of the marketing methods you have used to source customer traffic?

f. In your present position, how do you stay current with market and industry trends? Give me an example.

g. What is your approach to networking? Tell me how you utilized networking in your last position to generate customer leads.

h. In your last position, how did you determine how many new contacts and customer appointments you had to make each month?

i. Who is your mentor/subject matter expert at work? Tell me about the last time you asked this person for advice. How do you learn from them?

Leadership Questions

13) Vision

    a.   How do you keep your team focused on your department's goals?

    b.   A good leader leads by example. Can you tell me about a time when you have led by example?

    c.   Give me an example of how you have inspired your work team.

    d.   Tell me about a time when you took the initiative to lead your team on a new task.

    e.   With your current team, can you tell me how you balance the priorities of your team vs. the priorities of other departments?

    f.   How do you align your unit's goals with the strategic direction of the organization?

    g.   What have you done to ensure that your employees understand how their work relates to the overall objectives of the business?

14) Performance Management

    a. Tell me about a time when you used the disciplinary process which resulted in the termination of employment for someone in your department.

    b. Can you give me an example of how you have managed the performance of one of your employees?

    c. Can you give me an example of how you have managed the performance of your work team?

    d. What was one of the worst problems with a team you supervised? How did you work with your team to overcome this situation?

    e. Can you tell me how you recognize and reward employees?

    f. How have you managed the morale and motivation of your employees? Your work team?

15) <u>Employee Development</u>

a. Give me an example of a time when you taught an employee to improve his or her judgment and make independent decisions.

b. How have you developed others to take responsibility and make decisions?

c. How have you encouraged an employee to resolve problems on his or her own?

d. Tell me about an employee who exceeded expectations because you assisted his or her development. What did you do?

e. How have you included employee development in your performance appraisals?

16) Team Building

a. How have you encouraged a team to resolve problems on its own?

b. How have you responded when team members have come to you with suggestions for improvement?

c. Tell me about a large disagreement you had within a work team. How did you resolve it?

d. How have you managed a work team through the "storming" stage of development?

e. When you took responsibility for a new work team, how did you assess its level of development?

f. With a new work team, what did you do to help it quickly and successfully move through the "forming" stage?

g. Can you tell me about a time when you had to insert a new employee into a well-developed work team? How did you ensure that the team would keep performing at a high level?

h. In the work team you are currently managing, how have you worked with individual employees to improve the overall performance of the team?

CHAPTER 9: Let's take a BetterView

In the previous chapters we learned about all the different types of interviewing techniques in use today. We covered job match, traditional, and behavioral interview questions in depth. These are the same topics most other interviewing skills books teach. Now it is time for us to go beyond these expected topics and advance your understanding of what is actually happening during an interview. With a new perspective, you can develop new interviewing skills and techniques to truly stand out.

Companies are Seeking Superior Talent

For any organization, in any industry, superior talent is the greatest competitive advantage. The companies that hire the best people consistently perform better. With the best employees, companies can operate with a lower headcount and still have superior sales, innovation, customer service, quality, and cost control, while at the same time these employees drive a positive workplace culture with employee satisfaction. In short, every aspect of a company is better when you hire superior talent. The opposite is also true; the cost of hiring inferior candidates can send a company into bankruptcy.

These statements about the impact of superior talent are common sense, and there are numerous examples of companies succeeding or failing because of the quality of their workforce. Every CEO speaks about the need for a better workforce. The challenge for company owners and hiring managers is figuring out how to obtain better people than their competition. Companies have instituted countless initiatives to improve, attract, and retain talent such as training programs, benefits, education assistance, ping pong tables, free coffee, "bring your pet to work day," etc. While all these programs are nice, at the end of the day, there is only one solution to obtain better talent. The only way to obtain superior talent is to hire the best people and not hire the others. This means that companies must have a superior interview selection process for long-term success.

It's that simple. Hire the best people and do not hire the others. It doesn't cost anything extra to hire the best people; the hiring manager just needs to know how to interview accurately. With this simple, powerful rule driving the success or failure of a company, you would think that the practice of interviewing would have been perfected by now.

The Practice of Interviewing

The practice of interviewing was initiated long ago as the method used by hiring managers to determine who would be hired. After hundreds of years and millions of interviews, companies have now instilled the interview as the accepted and expected requirement to entry. This habitual question and answer exchange between interviewer and interviewee has become so ingrained that it can even be described as a custom or a ritual in today's society.

After all this time, isn't it astounding that job interviews at most companies are still so basic, vague, and inaccurate? This deficiency can be viewed in the same way as the large number of people called supervisors who lack supervisory skills. This thing we refer to as an "interview" has evolved little over many years, and remains mostly misunderstood by hiring managers and even more so by job seekers. Now, there have been some good methods developed, such as behavioral interviewing, which has substantially improved the process. But unfortunately, most hiring managers and job seekers haven't learned how to properly use this skill yet. The development of interviewing has also been limited because there are no standards, few classes teach interviewing skills, and anyone is free to become an interviewer or recruiter.

Insanity can be defined as doing the same thing over and over while expecting different results. Some companies believe that they can make a more accurate hiring decision by requiring the candidate to interview numerous times with multiple interviewers. While a more thorough interview is helpful, just doing more of the same thing over and over with an insufficient approach is a wasted effort.

Most hiring managers, as well as most job seekers, have just accepted interviewing in its current, limited state. This is like using the wrong club on the golf course. You may eventually put the golf ball in the hole, but there will be a lot of unnecessary bad shots along the way. In order for you to ensure success in your interview, you will need to move beyond the current paradigm of interviewing. You need to find a different approach to your interview. You need to consider that interviewing can actually be more science than art.

Interviewing should be considered a practice, in a similar way that a lawyer practices law, or a doctor practices medicine, or a baseball player practices hitting, fielding, and pitching. Mickey Mantle, one of the greatest baseball players of all time once said, "It's unbelievable how much you don't know about the game you have been playing your entire life."

Let's Take a BetterView

Your challenge, and your opportunity, is to advance your understanding of the practice of interviewing. You will need to open your mind to a new perspective of what is actually happening during an interview. Once you adjust your perspective, you will find that the more you learn about interviewing, the more you will come to understand that there is still more to know.

There is more to doing well in your interview beyond just knowing how to answer some of the common interview questions. Behavioral interviewing is clearly an advancement beyond the traditional interview questioning technique, but something is still missing. It is an inadequate approach to fully evaluating a candidate. Hiring managers want more out of a candidate.

Hiring managers consistently hire the candidates they "like." They hire the candidates who project charisma and talent. They want to "feel" confident that you are a superior performer. This is what they are referring to when they ask for a "well-rounded candidate." They need to be impressed and excited about you. They want a candidate with "Star Quality." They want "WOW!" Hiring managers require these positive impressions from you, even if they can't quantify what "WOW" really looks like.

73

This means that you, the job seeker, can study and prepare your answers to the job match, traditional, and behavioral interview questions, but just having the correct answers will still be insufficient. The hiring manager will evaluate HOW you answer every question. Hiring managers will attempt to determine if you are a fit for their needs. When their questions are insufficient, it is important for you to understand that this gap will be filled with their feelings and perceptions about you. This is when HOW you answer a question becomes important.

You need to accept that there is a gap in the hiring manager's understanding of you that cannot be answered through any of the interviewing techniques in use today. So how do you fill this gap in understanding? How do you address these feelings and perceptions the hiring manager has unknowingly developed about you? How do you take control of this situation and control the impressions developing in the interviewer's mind?

What in the heck is a "Gut Feeling?"

Let's break away from an incorrect, commonly held paradigm and take a BetterView of what is actually happening during an interview. It is time to look into that vague term called a "gut feeling."

Here is a common definition of "Gut Feeling":

> *An instinct or intuition, an immediate or basic feeling as opposed to an opinion based on facts.*

Most people who I have spoken with would consider this to be a sufficient definition, but I disagree. Just because something is hard to define, that doesn't mean it is undefinable. This commonly held belief, this paradigm, is not accurate, and this lack of understanding has led to confusion and poor interviews being conducted by hiring managers, as well as a sense of helplessness by job seekers.

A "feeling" about a person is not immediate; it is actually a reaction. Our senses first need to receive at least some type of information before they can be evaluated by our instincts, intuition, experience, or pre-conceived notions. A "gut feeling" IS a reactionary opinion based upon facts. It is just that these facts sensed are initial, incomplete, and biased by our pre-conceptions. Do you agree with these statements? If so, congratulations; you have just broken out of this paradigm! Now, let's define what is actually happening.

Here is a more accurate definition of "Gut Feeling":

> *A gut feeling is a reactionary thought based upon pre-conceived notions or biases used to quickly evaluate initial, probably incomplete, information received from one's senses.*

Accepting this new definition, we can state that an interviewer's gut feeling about you, the job seeker, is actually a reactionary thought. It is based on what they sense from you. It is a thought originating from what they see, what they hear, and what they smell. Now that you have a clearer understanding of how a "gut feeling" is created, this means that you can take control of many of these factors and greatly influence an interviewer's gut feelings.

So let me simply restate our new paradigm:

> *You can greatly control an interviewer's gut feeling about you.*

The key is learning the common positive and negative pre-conceptions or biases, and then adjusting your behavior to send the signals supporting these positive gut feelings. It is that simple, and you control most of what is happening.

Making an Impression in Your Interview

Everyone has heard the saying that it is important to make a good first impression. While it is a critical aspect to an interview, I think we can all agree that these same people fail to follow up this statement by defining exactly what making a good first impression really means. Even more vague is understanding how an impression is actually formed in the interviewer's mind. This lack of clarity leads to the void being filled with feelings, nebulous expressions, and the default judgment that

75

interviewing is an art and can't be defined. I consistently hear meaningless comments when it comes to evaluating candidates, such as:

- ❖ "The hiring manager will only give a job offer to a person she likes."
- ❖ "What kind of impression did he make?"
- ❖ "How did you feel about the candidate?"
- ❖ "What kind of impact did she make?"
- ❖ "He seemed persuasive."
- ❖ "I liked her energy."

Whenever I have debriefed with hiring managers after an interview, the discussion inevitably comes around to these intangible attributes ascribed to the candidate. In other words, how did this candidate make them feel? What kind of impression did they make? Then once the hiring managers have stated their feelings about a candidate, what proceeds next are attempts to justify these feelings. They do this by taking the candidate's answers from other interview questions and transfer these pieces to the desired attributes. This is not an intentional approach by the hiring managers. I would describe it more so to be a syndrome where an attempt is made to be accurate but the methodology is insufficient. Throughout my career I have worked with very different types of companies, including some with intricately designed interview processes that attempt to eliminate as much of this type of error as possible, but this flawed approach still exists and remains an important aspect to every interview. At the same time, you also need to understand that the impressions you project are an important part of who you are, especially for client-facing positions in careers such as sales or customer service, so employers really should be evaluating and selecting based upon these attributes.

Let me state this again- Just because something is hard to define, that doesn't mean it is undefinable. Terms such as "gut feeling" and "first impression" are vague and misused, but it is clear that impressions are a very important aspect to being successful in an interview.

Hiring Managers Want to be Impressed

As an in-house HR manager, and then again as an outside third-party recruiter, I learned quickly that hiring managers were selecting candidates based upon attributes beyond the job requirements. They desired candidates they "liked," and they needed confidence that these same people would be superior performers in their jobs. They would come to me and describe the "candidate profiles" needed for candidates to be successful in their departments. The attributes they described were mostly vague descriptions of likeable, hardworking people. The candidates they hired were the ones who produced the best "gut feel." They consistently desired candidates with charisma and perceived talent.

This forced me to define what these hiring managers really meant by their term "gut feeling." I needed to take these descriptions of the personalities and attributes they desired and learn what to look for from candidates which evoked these feelings. This led me to define the many impressions made by candidates during interviews and identify the signs candidates were projecting to make these impressions.

Throughout the interviews, from before the introduction to after the closing, I found that candidates projected signs that formed numerous impressions. Whether they were answering a traditional interview question or a behavioral question, they were always creating impressions. These impressions added emphasis, color, energy, and emotion to statements. These impressions are critically important to your success because they impact the way the interviewer feels about you. These impressions create the "WOW" factor the interviewer is looking for from you.

What is needed is a way for you to understand these impressions and control them in your interview. In the next chapter you will learn about Impression Interviewing™, which will provide the understanding to project positive impressions.

CHAPTER 10: Introducing Impression Interviewing™

Let's take a BetterView to clearly understand what happens when an impression is made. In this chapter I will break down and define some of the different types of impressions. Then I will share a new approach, called Impression Interviewing, that will provide clarity about the signs you can send to project each of these different impressions. You will find that you can practice, develop, and control these signs. By using this approach, you will learn to project each of the impressions that go into making a "first" as well as a "lasting" impression in your interview.

What is an Impression?

Let's define what "making an impression" means for the purpose of impression interviewing:

> *An Impression can be described as a feeling of greatness that is projected by a job candidate and perceived by the interviewer.*

An impression always begins with a projection initiated by the candidate. These are signals you send in verbal and nonverbal ways. Even before the first question is asked in the interview, you project impressions through numerous signals such as your correspondence, the way your resume is written, your attire, your walk, and your physical appearance. During the interview, an impression can be described as HOW you answer a question, not the answer itself.

Impressions fill the absences and deficiencies in an interviewer's understanding of a candidate. When an interviewer first meets a candidate, impressions will be formed in his mind before any conversation occurs. Impressions dominate the initial thoughts of the interviewer, until some of them can be replaced by answers from the candidate on the long list of job requirements. Interviewers use their questions to obtain factual data to replace their initial impressions of you, so as the interview progresses, a good interviewer should be able to obtain factual data on all the job requirements and competencies needed for the position. However, an interview is never a perfect method of assessment. There will always be some deficiency in the interviewer's understanding of you that cannot be answered through any of the interviewing techniques in use today. There will also be a first impression bias influencing the interview. Where the interviewer's questions are insufficient, it is important for you to understand that this gap will be filled with their feelings and perceptions about you. This is when HOW you answer a question becomes important.

Impressions add meaning and emphasis to your statements. This is done through techniques such as word choice, controlling the pace and tone of your voice, eye contact, hand movements, and changes in your posture. You project feeling and emotion through the impressions you send, whether or not your projections are intentional.

Impressions give an interviewer the appearance or perception of how well you will perform in a job. For example, a person who is soft spoken and lacks eye contact will be perceived as a lower performer as compared to another candidate with a louder voice and strong eye contact. This perception may or may not be accurate; it is just how the interviewer feels. An impression is based upon a reactionary thought, from the signs you project, in the same way as a "gut feeling." An interviewer is going to assign his personal beliefs, experiences, and assumptions to the impression signs you are sending. You need to recognize that this bias still exists, but in an interview this bias is almost always toward the most socially accepted norms.

By using impression interviewing techniques, you can greatly influence the interview because you control all the signals being sent. The impressions you project allow you to fill the interviewer's gap in understanding and add emphasis to all your answers to interview questions. The impressions you project create the feelings and perceptions the interviewer is unknowingly developing about you. With this awareness, you can also observe the responses you receive from the interviewer to help you understand how to adjust your approach throughout the conversation.

It is helpful to understand that in an interview there are multiple impressions being received by the interviewer, not just one unique impression. Let me explain…. It is very common after your interview to be asked the question, "So what type of impression did you make?" This is actually an extremely vague question! Are you being asked about your friendliness? Your politeness? The confidence you projected? Your ability to be a good co-worker? Your handshake? Your concise answers to questions? Your preparation? The energy in your walk? The pace of your speech? The thoughtfulness of the questions you asked? Your eye contact? As you will see, these are all very different types of impressions, and only when they are considered separately can an accurate answer be obtained. Unfortunately, in the world we live in now, most interviewers combine everything together to form an "overall impression," which is just a mixed bag of feelings and perceptions.

Many different attributes and skills can be projected to create impressions, so let's further define what is meant when we refer to impressions.

> *There are different types of impressions- They include traits, attributes, personalities, skills, or competencies, projected by a job candidate and perceived or felt to exist by an interviewer.*

It is important to clarify that an impression is different from what many people would describe as a competency. An impression is actually the feeling or perception of a competency, not the competency itself. For example, someone who is talkative may be perceived to have good customer service skills, without ever providing a situational example where they have demonstrated the customer service competency in the past. In previous chapters, the behavioral interviewing approach has been presented because it is the most effective tool utilized by interviewers to assess competencies.

Now you understand impressions and how they are different from competencies. You also understand that there are many different types of impressions.

Observable Signs

A job seeker projects an impression through observable signs. Similar to the way behavioral signs show the existence of a competency, observable signs project impressions.

Observable signs send impressions to an interviewer that a competency exists.

The difference is that these impressions are only feelings or perceptions that a competency exists, not the competency itself.

These signs you project are generated from a combination of verbal and nonverbal communication methods. You constantly project observable signs through your appearance, eyes, smile, posture, walk, hand gestures, voice, actions, and speech.

Let's look at an example. In the chapter on behavioral interviewing, we presented many examples of behavioral signs describing the persuasiveness competency in salespeople. In a similar way, we can also identify observable signs to project the impression that a person is persuasive.

Think of a typical persuasive salesperson. What is your perception of how they look? How they talk? How they move? Write down your answers to these questions.

Your answers have combined to create your own personal, biased profile of a persuasive salesperson. Now, here are some other common "observable signs" used to describe a persuasive salesperson: Polished attire, polished appearance, firm handshake, talkative, quickly transitions from formal to friendly/casual speech, uses colorful or impactful wording, high energy in voice, fast pace of speech, leans into your personal space, asks a lot of questions, drives the direction of the conversation, expressive hand gestures, smiles frequently, strong eye contact. How many of these signs fit your biased profile?

I think you will agree that none of these 14 observable signs factually point to the existence of a persuasive salesperson. However, these observable signs do send the impression that this person is persuasive. After this first impression, the interviewer will be inclined to favor this candidate throughout the remainder of the interview.

An Observable Sign can make Multiple Impressions

When an interviewer perceives an observable sign, it can influence his feelings about one or more than one impression. For example, when a job seeker wears polished, conservative attire for an interview, he is sending only one observable sign, but the interviewer perceives this sign in a positive way toward multiple impressions. Positive perceptions are made by the interviewer about the job seeker's professionalism, confidence, competence, socialization skills, style, healthy appearance, and integrity.

Impression Categories

Let's identify some of the different types of impressions by separating them into logical groups. We can easily separate impressions into many different categories, or families. One approach is to focus on the impressions most important to your interview. Hiring managers desire to hire someone they "like" and they want to have confidence that this same person will be a superior performer. Therefore, we will group our impressions into different categories based upon impressions projecting Charisma and Talent. These impression categories can be defined as:

> **Charisma**- Impressions that project compelling attractiveness, personality, and emotion.

> **Talent**- Impressions that project ability, competence, and potential for superior performance.

In the next sections we will list our Job Seeker's Impression Model, with 9 impressions organized by these Charisma and Talent categories. Each impression will be listed with its definition, sample observable signs used to project the impression, and the competencies influenced by the impression. The first category is impressions showing Charisma. The second category is impressions for Talent. Then the third category is impressions with aspects of both Charisma and Talent. Here are the 9 impressions:

The Job Seeker's Impression Model:

Impressions showing Charisma
1) Friendly
2) Genuine

Impressions showing Talent
3) Energetic
4) Perceptive
5) Intelligent
6) Prepared

Impressions showing both Charisma & Talent
7) Confident
8) Ethical
9) Optimistic

Charisma Impressions

1) Friendly
Definition- Behaves in a pleasant, kind, polite, and respectful manner; makes others feel comfortable.

Observable Signs- Recognize and greet others; approachable; make small talk; transition your approach and words from initially formal to familiar casual as the interview progresses; open doors for others; say please and thank you; use proper etiquette; use appropriate language; make simple and polite jokes; avoid sarcasm; smile frequently; energy in voice, pace is upbeat; volume in voice is slightly higher than normal; eyes are wide and bright; frequent eye contact; use positive expressive hand gestures. These observable signs project impressions endorsing character, adaptability, customer service, relationship building.

2) Genuine

Definition- Shows openness; sincere, receptive, honest, candid, or authentic.

Observable Signs- Selectively share personal examples to support discussion topic; selectively share topics from family or childhood; acknowledge when others are being genuine; direct eye contact when discussing genuine topic; pace of voice is steady with volume lower than normal; posture is relaxed; arms are open with slow movements. These observable signs project impressions endorsing communication, adaptability, character, and especially relationship building.

Talent Impressions

3) Energetic

Definition- Projects drive, emotion, and ability to get results.

Observable Signs- Wide and bright eyes; strong eye contact; strong and positive tone in voice; pace of speech changes to show emphasis and emotion; posture frequently leaning forward; powerful hand gestures; provide examples of resilience, work ethic, challenge, achievement, and drive. These observable signs project impressions endorsing performance, communication, and leadership, especially results.

4) Perceptive

Definition- Observant and sensitive to surroundings; actively listens to confirm meaning; adept at noticing obscure information; identifies possible outcomes in advance.

Observable Signs- Ask questions to verify understanding; anticipate the next question or next steps to help the interview flow; make perceptive comments from company research and tour of facility; calm and quiet while eyes scan and change focus. These observable signs project impressions endorsing vision and problem solving, especially tactical thinking.

5) Intelligent

Definition- Shows sound reasoning, judgment, and common sense; shows ability to learn; forms conclusions in a logical and reasonable way.

Observable Signs- Look for opportunities to ask thoughtful questions; ask thoughtful questions and make common sense conclusions from company research; mention using common sense and logical thought process; acknowledge common sense and conclusions of others; make wrap-up statements; share examples of how you have learned or been recognized for learning or meaningful decisions; share examples of being expert in your field; eyes look up or away thoughtfully; hand gestures touching chin and head. These observable signs project impressions endorsing problem solving and leadership, especially decision making.

6) Prepared

Definition- Shows clear and definite focus, concentration, and purpose toward the company and position; shows anticipation and planning; projects effort to make ready beforehand; properly equipped and willingness to interview.

Observable Signs- Strong, focused eye contact; stay on topic; at attention; give concise responses; thoroughly prepared for interview; evidence of advanced company research. These observable signs project impressions endorsing leadership and performance, especially planning and results.

Charisma and Talent Impressions

7) Confident

Definition- Shows poise, aura, control, and a presence without being boastful or egotistical.

Observable Signs- Thoroughly prepared for interview; shows eagerness or takes initiative to move to the next step in the conversation; answer without pause or with short, thoughtful pause; give concise and efficient answers; provide examples where you have taken initiative in the face of opposition;

firm handshake; eyes are wide and bright; frequent eye contact, especially when speaking about the important or genuine parts of a topic; ease of walk with full, effortless steps; chin up; smile often, with expressions supporting discussion topic; energy in voice, pace is steady and upbeat; volume in voice is mostly slightly higher than normal, change volume in voice lower when serious and higher when excited about topic; use positive expressive hand gestures to support words; posture is mostly upright, lean forward when speaking about important topics; show calmness and stillness when others are talking. These observable signs project impressions endorsing leadership, vision, performance management, decision making, problem solving, persuasiveness, relationship building, self-confidence, character, and resilience competencies.

8) Ethical

Definition- Trustworthy, professional, shows loyalty to employer, conforms to commonly held standards of conduct, exhibits a courteous, conscientious, and businesslike manner in the workplace.

Observable Signs- Arrive on time; keep conversation positive; speak positively about previous boss and job; be approachable; open posture; open hand gestures; facial expressions somewhat serious when discussing ethics topics; pace of voice is steady with volume lower than normal; acknowledge and respect confidentiality; keep topics work appropriate; provide examples where you have been loyal to your employer; provide examples where you have approached undesirable tasks positively, provide examples showing respect for rules; conservative attire; speech avoids slang and profanity. These observable signs project impressions endorsing performance, communication, and leadership competencies, especially character.

9) Optimistic

<u>Definition</u>- Controls emotions to remain hopeful and emphasize positive comments, responses, and solutions; proactively identify and plan for future problems.

<u>Observable Signs</u>- Thoroughly prepared for interview; bring extra copies of resume; ask about challenges to anticipate in this new position; make statements seeing the best in other people, situations, or events; provide examples of strong prevention and proactiveness; provide examples of encouragement and motivation of others; eyes are wide and bright; direct eye contact; pace and tone of voice change to support talking points; active and positive hand gestures to support talking points. These observable signs project impressions endorsing performance, decision making, relationship building, and team building, especially planning and results.

Samples of Common Observable Signs

There are endless ways for you to project observable signs for these impressions, and as discussed previously, each of these signs creates one or multiple impressions in the mind of the interviewer. This section presents a number of common observable signs to use before, during, and after the interview. These methods can be used for both charisma and talent impressions. You may not realize it, but you are sending multiple impressions prior to your actual interview. Because these are the initial impressions received by the interviewer, these are also some of the most important observable signs for you to project! Here are some of the common methods for you to project observable signs before, during, and after your interview:

<u>Online Presence</u>
Your profiles and posts found online such as Facebook, Twitter, or LinkedIn.

Observable Signs- Photos and subject matter show good judgment; solid writing skills; refrain from profanity; show positive socialization and relationships with friends and family; project good morals and ethics.

<u>Written Materials</u>
This includes your resume and other items prepared for the interview such as application, reference list, project list, and folio.

Observable Signs- Logical polished format/layout; correct spelling; consistent punctuation and capitalization; proper grammar; show eloquence and project strong positive energy through wording and sentence structure; easy to read with balanced use of white space; clearly show contact information; no errors. Resumes should clearly state responsibilities held; show strengths and achievements; use action words; be written for the specific position to which you are applying.

<u>Phone Calls & Correspondence</u>
Verbal and written communication by phone, email, text, or mail. Examples include emails and calls to schedule interviews, thank-you-notes, and follow-up correspondence.

Observable Signs- Timely; responsive; tone is initially polished and professional then gradually becomes more friendly and casual in subsequent communications; attention to format, spelling, and punctuation.

Physical Appearance
The outward look of a person, not including body language or dress style.

Observable Signs- High standard of personal hygiene; well groomed; healthy appearance; conservative makeup; minimal perfume or cologne.

Clothing Style
The design of a person's attire.

Observable Signs- Polished; appropriate for the situation and current fashion; colors and patterns that do not distract; also includes shoes, coat, purse, portfolio, pen, or any other items carried into the interview.

Body Language
Physical movements and gestures, including eyes, smile, walk, handshake, hand gestures, and posture.

Observable Signs- Open and bright eyes showing energy and excitement; eye contact to support topics; frequent smiles to support positive topics; head up and in the direction of the person talking or leading the discussion; firm handshake; facial expressions supporting the energy or tone of conversation; walk with purpose, confidence and ease; proper posture with changes to support speech; gestures used to support speech.

Pace of Speech
The rate and tempo of speaking.

Observable Signs- Normally a steady pace, flowing with an upbeat speed; pace increases to support the energy or positive excitement in a conversation; pace slows to support seriousness of a topic.

Tone of Speech
Pitch, volume, energy, and strength of speaking.

Observable Signs- Project energy through tone; during interview tone should be stronger than normal with conviction; pitch increases to support the energy or positive excitement in a conversation; pitch lowers to support seriousness of a topic.

Grammar
Structure, arrangement, phrasing, and usage of words to create well-formed sentences.

Observable Signs- In both verbal and written communications, ensure proper sentence structure and word usage; as communications progress, the use of grammar should change from formal to become more casual and friendly; use consistent punctuation and capitalization in written communications.

Eloquence
Fluent use of words to express oneself clearly and with impact; adjust wording to the audience.

Observable Signs- In both verbal and written communications; use appropriate slang for the industry; show better than expected command of language through the use of descriptive and impactful wording and sentence structure to support discussion topics.

Important Considerations for Impression Interviewing

Impressions toward charisma and talent are absolutely needed in order for you to create that "WOW" factor that is so important in hiring decisions. The impressions you create make you memorable and separate you from other equally qualified candidates.

Projecting strong, positive energy is one of the most powerful observable signs, and it is one of the easiest to project through your eyes and voice.

In today's world everyone can be found on the internet, so you need to control the impressions you are projecting through your online profiles. Let hiring managers find respectable pictures and posts projecting maturity and good judgment. Clean up your post history from when you were younger and lacked solid judgment.

A resume needs to project your polish, achievements, and talent. Everyone has heard about the need to prepare a professional resume, so you would think that this wouldn't be an issue. However, the vast majority of resumes project insufficient impressions. Most of the resumes I have reviewed need significant improvement, so do not just assume that your resume is fine. You should have at least two HR professionals help you to improve your resume. Resumes need a logical format, should be easy to read with a balanced use of white space, clearly show contact information, contain no errors, clearly state responsibilities held, show strengths and achievements, use action words, and be written for the specific position to which you are applying.

Most candidates are too casual during initial contact. When an interviewer makes initial contact with you to schedule an interview, the way you respond by phone or email will be extremely influential. This is where you transition from a resume to a person, in the mind of the interviewer. The message on your phone's voicemail needs to be professional, polished, and genuine, with positive energy in your voice. When you respond, be polite and respectful, with positive energy in your voice! Initial email correspondence needs to be written in complete sentences, with proper grammar and spelling. Include a "Respectfully" or "Thank you" with your signature line at the end of your email. Use this same approach even if your initial contact is through texting. Remember that you aren't communicating with a familiar friend;

you are forming a first impression in the mind of the interviewer with every little thing you say and do.

Ease of scheduling interviews is also impactful. Respond promptly to any messages. With today's technology, it is expected that you respond the same workday or at least within 24 hours. The interviewer has contacted you to schedule an interview, so you need to make yourself available. If you can't interview at the time requested, then express your interest and offer reasonable alternative interview times in your response. Try to save the interviewer time by minimizing the number of instances she needs to contact you to schedule an interview. Excessive messages, delays, and difficulties from you send the impression that you lack professionalism and respect. You are also projecting that you will be difficult to work with, disorganized, and inefficient.

Rating Your Impression Performance

Now that you have a good understanding of the different types of impressions projected during an interview, the next step is to learn your strengths and weaknesses in how your impressions are perceived. We will do this through the use of a rating scale. Interviewers frequently use rating scales to evaluate candidates on whatever factors or competencies they are evaluating for their position, so this will be a helpful learning exercise.

Using the rating scale below, begin this process by rating yourself on how good you think you are at projecting each of these impressions. After you have rated yourself on each of these impressions, identify the impressions most important for your upcoming interview. Each position has a different mix of impressions needed. For instance, the desired impressions for an accountant are very different from those for a marketing representative.

To achieve an even more accurate view as to how you rate with these impressions, you also need to ask others to rate you. You need to find a few people who know you well and will provide honest, constructive feedback. When you compare their ratings to your self-evaluation, you will identify the difference between how you think you come across to others and how you are actually perceived.

Impression Rating Scale

1) **Weakness**- Glaring flaw or drawback with impact, possible deal-breaker, requires strengths in other areas to overcome

2) **Deficient**- Mildly negative to negative

3) **Need More Information**- Additional information should be obtained to rate as deficient or sufficient

4) **Sufficient**- Mildly positive to positive

5) **Strength**- Excels with impact, star quality, will provide the ability to overcome other possible areas of weakness

Rate Your Impressions Below:

Impression - Friendly
1. Weakness
2. Deficient
3. Need More Information
4. Sufficient
5. Strength

Impression - Genuine
1. Weakness
2. Deficient
3. Need More Information
4. Sufficient
5. Strength

Impression - Energetic
1. Weakness
2. Deficient
3. Need More Information
4. Sufficient
5. Strength

Impression - Perceptive
1. Weakness
2. Deficient
3. Need More Information
4. Sufficient
5. Strength

Impression - Intelligent
1. Weakness
2. Deficient
3. Need More Information
4. Sufficient
5. Strength

Impression - Prepared
1. Weakness
2. Deficient
3. Need More Information
4. Sufficient
5. Strength

Impression - Confident
1. Weakness
2. Deficient
3. Need More Information
4. Sufficient
5. Strength

Impression - Ethical
1. Weakness
2. Deficient
3. Need More Information
4. Sufficient
5. Strength

Impression - Optimistic
1. Weakness
2. Deficient
3. Need More Information
4. Sufficient
5. Strength

How can you Develop & Improve your Impressions?

All these observable signs sent to create your impressions are done with skills you can develop, so you can absolutely improve how you project yourself to interviewers. You will also find that as you develop these skills, you will positively impact the impressions being perceived in all the other relationships in your life. Your family, friends, and colleagues will notice the change and they will perceive your charisma and talent differently.

To improve your impressions, begin by studying each of the impressions in depth in order to gain a more thorough and comprehensive understanding of this approach. Then identify observable signs you can improve or add to your skill set. Practice sending these observable signs on a regular basis to prepare in advance for your next interview.

Another method to develop your impressions is to identify superior performers. These superior performers are experts at projecting the observable signs you would like to master. By observing, asking questions, and discussing these communication techniques with superior performers, you will be able to identify exactly how to project the impressions you desire.

You can also develop your acting skills. The profession of acting can be described as telling a story, and in this case, the story is about you and your audience is the interviewer. You are telling the interviewer how much of a match you are for the position you desire. When actors take on new characters, they create new personalities by creating, practicing, and then projecting observable signs.

Career coaches are excellent resources to help develop your interviewing skills. They have a better understanding than most about the impressions and biases which occur during an interview, so they should be able to grasp the concepts of impression interviewing and become useful evaluators and trainers for you.

Lastly, an excellent way for you to develop your impressions is simply to gain practice by going on multiple interviews. Each interview is an opportunity for you to practice and learn more about a new company and yourself.

CHAPTER 11: Questions for you to be Prepared to Ask

The previous chapters of this book have examined the questions being directed at you in an interview and how you should respond. In this chapter, we will discuss the questions you can ask. This part of the interview is very important because when the interviewer asks if you have any questions, he has just given you an invitation to take control of the interview.

Why Prepare a List of Questions to Ask?

Preparing a typed list of questions to bring with you to the interview can serve many purposes. The first reason is to obtain information to help you decide if you really want to work for this company. You also want to know if your new boss's management style will be a match for you. Another use of questions is to tell the interviewer about you. It tells the interviewer that you have prepared. Your typed list shows that you have thought about the position and the company and what is important to you. It is an additional way for you to make a positive impression on your talent. Asking questions about expectations in the position or challenges the department is currently facing can give you information about what the interviewer is looking for and enable you to effectively present your background to meet these needs. You can use a question to shift the discussion to a topic the interviewer missed so you can emphasize a strength that hasn't already been presented. An example would be asking about the department's safety record to allow you to easily insert your past successes with safety programs. Here's another wonderful use- Asking for the interviewer's opinion on a topic shows that you value his opinion, builds respect and trust, and earns you bonus points on your charisma impressions.

As you can see, the use of questions provides a subtle tool to take control of the interview in many different ways. Your questions should be open-ended to allow a comfortable, free-flowing discussion. Now, how do you develop this list of questions?

Begin by Developing Your Strategy

Instead of just assembling a random list of questions to ask, you should first determine what information you need to get answered. This will provide the clear objectives for your research. But what information do you need?

Company Research

What do you want to know about the company you may be going to work for? You want to obtain information on the company's history, stability, senior managers, work culture, employee turnover, recent news, possible legal cases, lines of business, strengths and weaknesses, competitor strengths and weaknesses, and location of offices. Does this company have a good reputation in the community and its industry? Do they treat their employees well? A lot of this information can be obtained prior to your interview, so your questions for the interviewer on these topics should be used to show that you have done your research on the company. Your questions can be more specific to help you decide if you really do want to work there.

Position Research

You want to know if this job is going to be a match for you. What are the full job responsibilities and requirements? To whom does this position report? Are there any indirect reporting responsibilities as well? Does this position supervise others? If so, will you have full authority? Why is this job open? How does this position fit within the rest of your department?

New Boss Research

Any information to reveal your compatibility with your new boss and other members of the management team will be very helpful in determining if this job will be a match for you. What is this person's background and prior experience? What school did he attend? Does he have any unique interests? Does he belong to any associations? Is the job you are interviewing for only open because your potential new boss is an overbearing jerk and no one else wants to work for him? Or, does this person have a stellar reputation for developing and promoting talent? These are important questions you need to get answered before you accept an employment offer.

What is your strategy to make a positive impression with charisma and talent?
Just having a typed list of questions will project a positive impression. You can develop trust and openness by asking for the interviewer's opinion on topics. These topics shouldn't be too controversial, so asking speculative or hypothetical questions on the future of the position, department, or company will allow for a wide variety of answers. Look for topics with similar interests or passions with your interviewer.

How will you use questions to learn what the interviewer is looking for from you?
Asking for expectations and challenges within the position, department, and company will prompt many good questions and opportunities for you to handle any remaining concerns the interviewer may have.

How will you use questions to emphasize strengths and address weaknesses?
These questions can provide insight to what the interviewer thinks about you as a candidate. Always look for opportunities to address your weaknesses by applying strengths from other areas. Asking questions to uncover weaknesses or missing skills within the department or company will allow you to present your strengths in a way to fill these needs.

Where do you Search for Company Information?

Do not limit yourself to a quick internet search. There are too many other available sources where you can obtain insightful information. This is about your career, so take a little time to be thorough and learn from some different sources such as:

- ➢ Quarterly and annual shareholder reports of public companies
- ➢ Business credit reports
- ➢ Corporate and financial ratings from review companies
- ➢ Consumer protection government agencies
- ➢ Consumer protection organizations
- ➢ The company's website
- ➢ Internet search engines
- ➢ Online employee reviews of companies
- ➢ Company pages on social media
- ➢ Associations where the company is active
- ➢ Customers who purchase from the company
- ➢ Other companies who do business with the company

Your best information will come from current and former employees. Networking with your family, friends, and professional colleagues will always connect you with these employees. You will find most of them to be open and willing to provide insight to you about the position. Ideally, you also want to connect with people who are familiar with the person who will become your boss. Salespeople, customer service representatives, and any other employees who have outward facing positions are also good sources.

Your network of family, friends, and professional colleagues is your most powerful source. An efficient way to use your network is to develop a list of your 10 most networked people, obtain their email addresses, and ask them if you can contact them to assist with your job search. Then all you need to do is send a group email to your networking group and let them find the information sources for you!

Examples of Good Questions to Ask:

Questions about the Company & Position

1) What can you tell me about the company's history and senior managers that may not be common knowledge?

2) I understand your sales volume was x million last year and x million this year – to what do you attribute this growth?

3) What are the company's plans to improve its position in the market? New product lines?

4) How does this company compare with major competitors? Strengths and weaknesses?

5) How would you describe the company's culture? How does this match with the culture inside your department?

6) Does the company do performance reviews? How are they structured?

7) What are the current challenges faced by your department?

8) Describe the structure of the department and where I would fit.

9) What are the advantages and disadvantages of working at this company and in this particular position?

10) Describe your plans for this department over the next few years. What projects are upcoming? What would I be involved in?

11) What type of work/projects would I be responsible for in the first six months? The first year? After that?

12) If I started Monday, where would I be involved initially?

13) Why is this position open?

14) What are your initial expectations for me and what priorities would you like for me to focus on first?

15) What challenges will I face in this position?

16) What would a typical day involve? A typical week?

17) How will my progress be evaluated?

Questions about your Potential Boss

1) To whom does this position report?

2) How did you learn to manage others?

3) What is your style and philosophy of management? What style and philosophy is prevalent in management?

4) What is the turnover within this department?

5) How have you addressed performance issues in your department?

6) How would your employees describe you?

Questions to Emphasize your Strengths and Address Weaknesses
1) Can you define the specific problems/hurdles that need to be overcome by the candidate who accepts this position?

2) What are the three most important things you would need me to accomplish in the first year?

3) What kind of individual are you looking for? Personality? Work experience?

4) Looking at the current employees on your team, what skill set would you say is lacking or would be a beneficial addition?

5) How do my background and qualifications compare to other candidates who have been considered for this position?

6) Based on my background and skills, what might be my biggest difficulty?

Questions to Make a Positive Impression
1) How long have you been with XYZ company? What do you like most about this company? What do you like least?

2) Why did you join this organization?

3) How has your career progressed?

4) What do you see in the future for my position and this department?

What Questions should you NOT Ask?

Good judgment also requires that you know what questions and topics to avoid. The overall tone of the interview needs to remain positive, so try to keep your questions and the discussion as positive as possible.

While learning about your new boss's personality and management style are critical to your success, you need to be cautious to not drill your boss with too many questions. You do not want to challenge his management skills. Unfortunately, you can't get away with asking many behavioral interview questions to shed light on his skill set. The best managers will be open about themselves, so listen to how much and what they say without being prompted. You will also get a good feel for how much other employees respect the boss by observing their facial expressions and interactions. Ultimately, the best source of information on your future boss will come from your outside research.

You should also normally refrain from asking questions about salary, benefits, vacation, or other "me" questions, even if you are on your second or third interview. Unless the interviewer forces the discussion, these questions should be addressed only after you have received an employment offer. Once you have received a formal offer, the hiring manager has stated that he needs you to come to work for the company. This shifts your bargaining power from being just another candidate to being the person they have decided upon after exhausting the pool of available candidates and completing their interview process. This is the point in time when you are the most desirable, so this is the time when you have the most leverage to discuss pay and benefits.

CHAPTER 12: Strategies for Common Challenges

In this chapter we will look at some of the common challenges experienced by job seekers. From the perspective of having been inside the room where hiring decisions are made, I will provide some strategies for you by clarifying these challenges are and then offering approaches to overcome these challenges during your interview.

New Graduates with No Experience

Many new graduates express concern about their lack of experience and how they should address this topic during their interviews. The good news is that you do not need to be concerned about your lack of experience. If a hiring manager is interviewing you, then he has already made the decision that he is open to hiring a candidate without experience. You just need to understand how to address this concern when asked in the interview.

Many companies actually prefer to hire new graduates over those with previous job experience because they think that these new grads haven't developed bad habits from working at other companies. Please understand, I am not saying that this view is accurate; it is just a belief held by many hiring managers. The correct view is to understand that some candidates possess the adaptability competency while other candidates struggle with adapting. It is truly a question of an individual candidate's competency, not if they have prior job experience. These hiring managers who do not know how to interview for adaptability prefer to train new college graduates instead.

As a new graduate, you also have a unique advantage in interviews. It is more difficult for hiring managers to interview candidates without job experience because many of them lack the appropriate questions to ask. The most obvious questions come from looking at a resume and asking about previous job experience. However, in this situation interviewers need to know how to ascertain your ability to perform in the future, without the direct past experience. Therefore, in these interviews, if you know how to communicate your behavioral Situation – Action – Result answers to link your competencies to the required skills and responsibilities in the position, you will separate yourself from other candidates because of your ability to help the interviewer to clearly see your capabilities.

Your strongest approach to your interview is to come prepared with your list of situational examples and answer as many questions as possible with the behavioral Situation – Action – Result approach. Everyone has life experience. You just need to pull examples from multiple areas such as your college internships, your part-time jobs, your approach to school, sports teams, associations, and even your family life. Some of the more important competencies for you are the ability to learn, work ethic, results orientation, initiative, and team orientation. Most of these are competencies you were born with or developed at a young age.

Sales Job Seekers

A common challenge for sales candidates is that they rely too much on their persuasiveness and outgoing personalities, and they fail to fully prepare for the interview. I observed this often, even with polished and professional candidates. This may be because many salespeople lack strong planning and follow-up competencies. Many candidates I have interviewed cannot concisely tell me the steps in their sales process, and most forget to mention that closing the sale is the last and most important step! Preparation also means that you need to come to the interview ready to clearly emphasize your sales successes and achievements. An interviewer shouldn't have to ask follow-up questions to uncover that you were a five-time President's Club award winner.

The first step to being prepared is to know the sales process. There are a lot of variations out there on the sales process, but my recommendation is to keep it simple. For example, you can use these five steps: Develop trust, identify needs, present product/service to meet needs, overcome objections, and close the sale. You can also mention that after you close the sale, the sixth step is asking for referrals. Then, for each of these six steps you need to prepare your situational list of examples so you can give strong, positive stories about how you have implemented each of these steps with your customers.

Another recommended approach is to emphasize your sales successes and achievements. Create a bulleted list at the top of your resume entitled, "Sales Achievements." This list should include any awards or recognition such as President's Club, #2 of 50 Sales Representatives in the Region, and Best Sales Trainee. Also include performance such as, "Consistently achieved sales goals 8 quarters in a row," and "Ranked #3 out of 20 on National Sales Team." Then, come to the interview prepared to tell what you did differently from the other sales representatives to reach these achievements.

The truly superior salespeople brand themselves, are very competitive with themselves, strategically plan how they will present their product as compared to their competition, develop urgency, utilize referrals and references, develop a plan to follow up with customers, and when they hear "no," they are happy because they just uncovered another objection to overcome and close the sale. Be prepared with situational examples of how you have done all these things in the past. Important competencies for sales candidates are planning, follow-up, persuasiveness, resilience, competitiveness, and results.

Technical Job Seekers Lacking Interpersonal Skills

Everyone has a unique personality and there are many introverts or socially awkward people who have very capable technical skill sets. A large percentage of these folks work in the Science, Technology, Engineering, and Math (STEM) Industries. Unfortunately, many of these wonderful brainiacs and gear-heads of the world lack interpersonal skills, and this is a serious challenge when it comes to interviewing. If I am describing you, then you need to know that more and more hiring managers are demanding candidates who are "well-rounded." This means that they want to hire technical candidates who also excel with their interpersonal skills. Yes, even if you have a 4.0 GPA in engineering, this is a challenge for you to overcome.

So how do you show solid interpersonal skills in your interview? My recommendation is to use your problem solving competency, which is most likely one of your greatest strengths.

Start by going back and re-reading the chapters on impression interviewing. Then gather information to assess your charisma impressions by asking for feedback from your family and friends. Give yourself an honest rating on your charisma impressions so you have a clear understanding of what improvements are needed. Next, identify others who have strong interpersonal skills and outgoing personalities. Observe and talk with them to learn some of the specific things they do and say to make their impressions. You will be surprised to learn how simple and easy some of these techniques are once you focus your analytical skills. Then, add a few of these techniques to your interview. You will not need to be overly expressive in your approach; you just need to show that you can communicate and relate effectively enough with your co-workers and clients.

Managerial Job Seekers Lacking Supervisory Experience

This challenge is similar to the one faced by new graduates who lack work experience. In this same way, you should have confidence that if a hiring manager is interviewing you, then he has already made the decision that he is open to hiring a candidate without previous supervisory experience. Now let's look at some approaches to help you shine in the interview.

Your strongest approach to your interview is to come prepared with your list of situational examples from other parts of your life where you have displayed leadership and supervisory qualities, and then answer as many questions as possible with the behavioral Situation – Action – Result approach. Everyone has experience where they have held responsibility or influence over others. You just need to pull examples from other jobs, school projects, sports teams, associations or other groups. Some of the more important competencies here are vision, performance management, employee development, team building, ability to learn, planning, and results orientation.

If you are being promoted from within your work team, then you can expect to be asked about your ability to adjust from being a co-worker to a supervisor of your former co-workers. A nice response here is to emphasize and provide situational examples of how you are already recognized as an informal leader by your co-workers.

Job Seekers with a Felony or Misdemeanor Criminal Record

This is clearly a challenge, and many employers will never consider hiring a person with a criminal record. But have confidence, because times are changing on this subject. The First Step Act was recently passed in the United States, reducing the stigma and opening up new opportunities. It is becoming more common for companies to hire employees with criminal records. There are also new business owners and candidates running for political office who have been in your situation. You have enough options to be successful now. You only need one company to say "yes" and hire you! Then, once you develop a stable work history of being employed for a few years, it will become much easier for other employers to justify considering you.

Your greatest challenge will be getting your foot in the door for the interview, not the interview itself. So, you should begin by doing some research. You want to develop a list of companies that will most likely be open to employing candidates with criminal records. To find these companies you can contact employment assistance agencies and non-profit associations. Ask your friends and build your professional network of connected people. Also, feel free to call companies directly, talk with the receptionist, and ask if they will consider interviewing you. You may get referred to the HR department for an answer, or the receptionist may just give you an honest answer on the spot.

Your criminal record does need to be disclosed on the employment application. Briefly list what the charge was and then write that you "will discuss details during interview." On the employment application, there is normally a section at the bottom where you will be asked for your signature to confirm that the information you have written on your application is truthful, so be sure to not submit anything inaccurate. Then, in your interview you need to be genuine, honest, and straightforward, and confront this subject as soon as possible.

Once you have confirmed that the interviewer is open to listening, your approach to this challenge is very simple; tell the interviewer how you turned a weakness into a strength. Take responsibility for the crime and then tell how you addressed the remedies required by law. Then, state how you have matured and learned from this mistake. Finally, talk about how this incident has helped you to become stronger; you will never face a challenge as difficult as this in your new job and you have become a very resilient and humble person. The important competencies you need to focus on are resiliency, adaptability, and results.

Transitioning Military

Obviously, the transition from military to civilian life impacts your job search dramatically. The good news here is that your military training and culture have provided many strengths to utilize in your new job, and most interviewers assume that candidates coming from the military bring desirable competencies such as hard work, loyalty, ethics, resilience, results, and teamwork. There are also a few areas of concern you will need to focus on in your interview. There may be a concern with your ability to take initiative because you are coming from a strong chain of command environment. Also, the ability to exercise judgment in vague situations, and adaptability to different work styles and cultures will be challenges you need to be prepared to overcome in an interview.

The world of private business is unfortunately not as clear-cut as what you have become accustomed to in the military. Different companies as well as different industries will have a wide range of work cultures, so you should talk with other former military who have transitioned into the industry or type of position that you want to obtain. You will need to identify what type of work culture will be the best match for you.

On your resume and in your interview, you need to minimize the use of military jargon and acronyms. You also need to feel free to be more open, conversational, and persuasive during your interview. The social norms within the military are counter to the concept of selling. In the military you dealt more with absolutes and learned that misrepresentations and inaccuracies can cost lives. Civilians are much more willing and better accustomed to selling themselves, and you will need to take the initiative to develop professional relationships. No matter what you do when you leave the military, it is going to involve more sales and relationship development. The good news is that whether you realize it or not, you've had a fair amount of experience at it. You just may not have viewed it as selling. Some examples are advocating for why a subordinate deserves a promotion or getting buy-in from a team for a plan of action. However, in your interview, the sale that will be most essential in your transition will also feel the most awkward for you. You need to sell yourself.

Competencies to focus on are relationship building, persuasiveness, adaptability, initiative, decisiveness, and judgment.

Senior Job Seekers

Unfortunately, senior candidates face the most challenges in landing a new job. The greatest challenge is just getting your foot in the door to actually be interviewed. Then, a large list of topics are questioned such as the willingness to accept lower pay, willingness to take orders from a younger, less experienced manager, capability to adapt to a new work environment, energy to work at a fast enough pace, and ability to learn new technology and use computer software and hardware. These challenges need to be overcome by addressing them head-on and also emphasizing your strengths in other areas.

Because the greatest challenge will be obtaining the interview, you need to develop a list of companies that will most likely be open to employing senior candidates. Most of your job search time should be focused on expanding, developing, and utilizing your professional network to make connections within these companies. Obtaining an interview from a referral will be the most common source, and it just so happens that this will also be your best source for being able to obtain a job offer.

Prepare for your interview by developing your list of situational examples, and then answer as many questions as possible with the behavioral Situation – Action – Result approach. Examples need to be recent and focus on competencies such as energy, adaptability/change, job knowledge with new technology, the ability to learn, the ability to take initiative, and getting results.

In your interview, you need to take the initiative to bring up some important subjects. You both know that you are a senior candidate, but the interviewer will probably not mention anything because he doesn't want to get the company sued for age discrimination. Therefore, you need to be the one who speaks up about your age. Own it and talk openly about the necessary topics such as your willingness to accept lower pay if appropriate and take orders from a younger, less experienced manager.

Making a strong impression with your energy is very important, so be sure to project a high energy level throughout your interview. In addition to your energy, the talent impressions are also important for senior candidates to show. Important competencies for senior candidates include work ethic, adaptability, ability to learn new technology, teamwork, initiative, and results.

CHAPTER 13: Achieving your Primary Objectives

If you have read this far then you have put a lot of time and effort into your upcoming interview. You have also looked in-depth into the many different aspects of interviewing to obtain a BetterView of this process and learn skills needed to approach your interview with confidence.

Now, let's take a step back and look at the big picture again. You have read this material, completed your company research, typed your list of questions to ask the interviewer, and practiced and prepared your list of situational examples for the behavioral interview questions. You have also evaluated and developed your impression skills. Once you have finished these tasks, you will not need to worry about what questions may be coming because you will be the best prepared candidate entering the room. All you need to do now is focus on achieving your primary objectives.

Your Primary Objectives

When you enter your interview, your mind should be clear and focused on just a few of the most important objectives you want to accomplish. I call these your Primary Objectives:

Primary Objective #1
What is the most important thing you want the interviewer to know about you?

Primary Objective #2
What is a strength you can bring to separate you from other candidates?

Primary Objective #3
What is a weakness you need to address?

Primary Objective #4
Impress the interviewer by showing your charisma and talent.

Primary Objective #5
If you want this job, tell the interviewer that you are interested
and ask for the next step.

By keeping your focus on these primary objectives, you will have the clarity and confidence to let your charisma show and have fun during your interview! This really should be a fun and exciting experience for you. In your upcoming interview, you are being given the opportunity to advance your career, meet new people, learn about a new organization, brag a little about yourself, and most likely, receive a pay raise. What's not to like about that?

A Personal Note

Thank you so much for investing your time and effort with me to learn more about the practice of interviewing. I hope this material has challenged and inspired you to take control of your impressions and advance your interviewing skills.

Each time a successful match is made between a company and a new employee, it is an opportunity for both to progress. Companies grow and thrive when they hire the right talent, and at the same time, individuals are able to improve personally, experience success, and make a positive impact upon their family. My objective and desire is for you to experience this same success and positively impact your family.

Now that you have received all the information presented in this book, can you say that you have a BetterView of interviewing? If so, I would like to challenge you further by assisting others to advance their skills as well.

It's time for a BetterView.

Thanks for reading!

Please add a review on Amazon
and let me know what you thought.

Amazon reviews are extremely helpful for authors as well as other readers. Thank you for taking the time to support my work. Don't forget to share your review on social media with the hashtag #InterviewBetterView and encourage others to improve their interview skills!

Connect with Tom on:

Email: tfranke@RoundhouseRecruiting.com
LinkedIn: www.LinkedIn.com/in/tomfranke
Twitter: @RoundhouseJobs
Website: www.RoundhouseRecruiting.com